Happy New Year to
new friend Tony —
Donna McGill Miller

NAOMI'S STORY

BOEING'S ROSIE THE RIVETER

by Naomi Kalemjian

The cover picture shows Naomi's family about 1910. Naomi is seated on her father Harooteum Kalemjian's lap. Her mother Nooritza stands to her husband's left and in front (from left to right) is her brother Hurant, sister Anoosh, and another sister Loosaper. Two girls and a boy were born to the Kalemjian's after this photo was taken.

Copyright © 2005
by Garibaldi Books
710 Driftwood Ave.
Garibaldi, OR 97118
P.O. Box 283

All rights reserved. No part of the material protected by this copyright notice may be reproduced or utilized in any form or by any means, electronic or mechanical, including photocopying, recording or by any informational storage and retrieval system without written permission from the copyright owner.

ISBN: 0-9652434-4-3

Printed in the United States of America by
Maverick Publications • Bend, Oregon

Preface and Dedication

Each person has a life-story to tell. Fortunately Naomi wrote hers down. Once read it will not be forgotten. The loss of her family, her sad life with her aunt, and working at menial jobs, all makes it a sad story, but it has a happy note when she is attracted to Bernie Cohen and he to her. In Bernie she found the love she had so desperately sought since her tragic childhood in Marash, Turkey.

Naomi died on January 17, 1996. She entrusted our family with her memoirs hoping someday they might be inspirational to those Americans who have forgotten what a wonderful country ours is where even a little refugee girl can find happiness and love.

Bill and Kay McGill

Bernie and Naomi holding Naomi's God-daughter Suzanne McGill surrounded by McGill family members at the baby's Christening.

Publisher's Note

This book is dedicated to the Bill and Kay McGill family who were Naomi and Bernie's dear freinds. The McGill's remember both Naomi and Bernie fondly and were to the Cohens the family they never had. Suzanne McGill was Naomi's God-daughter and first transcribed Naomi's writings so this dedication is especially to her.

I became involved in helping publish *Naomi's Story* when I met Donna (McGill) Miller of Netarts, Oregon, at a Red Cross Blood Drive, and she invited me to read Naomi's writing. It is apparent that she wrote it over a period of many years starting with her earliest memories of Marash, Turkey, and ending when Bernie died in 1977. Although Naomi lived twenty years longer, her life story ends with Bernie's death.

Donna Miller and I when editing Naomi's writing made few changes. There were a few places where we made the verb tenses consistent with the past and present and two or three redundancies which sadly referred to her lost family. The organization of her book into parts corresponded to the challenges she faced at those times in her life and were very appropriate. She ends with *Epilogue, Feelings from My Heart* and *My Prayer*, which are fitting for Naomi was a person of great hope and faith who made the most of her life and enriched the lives of those around her.

Jack L. Graves
Garibaldi Books

Contents

PREFACE & DEDICATION: The McGill Family photo
PUBLISHER'S NOTE: Jack L. Graves, Garibaldi Books
PART I: Sad Memories that Live Forever 1
PART II: Oh Those Stormy Mistreatment Years 41
PART III: He Dried my Tears 48
EPILOGUE 68
FEELINGS FROM MY HEART 71
MY PRAYER 72
NAOMI'S ALBUM: Photographs Saved by Naomi 73
    Samples of Armenian orphan lace and weaving 73
    Naomi's citizenship paper 74
    Naomi with her cousins, her aunt and Miss Mather 75
    Naomi at her aunt's home 76
    Naomi as a young woman 77
    Naomi's wedding and invitation 78
    Naomi's wedding party and Bernie's poem 79
    Photos from Naomi's album 80
    Boeing goes to war 81
    Naomi's retirement party (from Boeing News) 82
    Naomi's retirement party, January 26, 1973 83
    Naomi mourns Bernie 84

PART I

Sad Memories that Live Forever

I remember too well. The year was 1917, and it happened in the little town of Marash, Turkey, in Asia Minor, where my entire family and I lived.

I sincerely believe in stating that my life has been tragic and strange, and yet the most interesting non-fiction story that I have ever read since my arrival to the United States in November, 1922. In reality, I have lived two very contrasting lives. One, in that semi-civilized, everlastingly accursed Turkey in Asia Minor, then a land of human slaughter, where for many generations two clashing religions, namely the Christians and the Mohammedans, otherwise the Armenians and the Turks respectively, were in constant turmoil. The other, my life in America, where the very height of civilization has been attained.

All my family and I were born in Marash, Turkey. Although many long, *and* torturous years have passed since that doomed day in June 1917, I still have a clear vision of the seven dear faces that have haunted me every day for these many years. There before my eyes stands my beloved mother, Nooritza Kalemjian, so tall and broad shouldered, with blue eyes, blonde hair and fair skin....not at all true to the Armenian's characteristic physical traits. My father Harooteun Kalemjian, rather small of stature, with dark brown hair and brown eyes, his hair turning gray at the temples. My oldest brother, Hurant, about 18 years old, already supporting the family by working in a bakery. Next was my oldest sister

Anoosh, 16 years old, ready to be married off as soon as my parents could find a suitable husband for her, as *was* the custom of the land. Then there was another sister named Loosaper, around 13 years old. I remember her being very sickly, and so died young. I was fourth in line, around eight years old at the time. My name is Naomi. Next was my little brother Meenas, about five years old, and another sister named Lootphia, three years old, lastly our baby sister also named Loosaper—in remembrance of our sister who had died, just months old *and* still breast feeding. We were all brunettes, with exception of my three-year-old sister who was like my mother—had blue eyes, blonde hair and fair skin. She was beautiful. Everyone loved and adored her. She was so different from the rest of us. The neighbors and the people on the street would stop and admire her with astonishment.

We were reasonably well to do but led a very simple life. Our home consisted of three modest rooms, two small ones and one full length which was used as a general hallway and was completely open on one side, facing the lower veranda. In one of the small rooms we kept hempen sacks full of staple foods, enough for a year's supply. We cooked our daily meals in the smokey fireplace at the far corner of that room. The second room served as a family den during the day, but in the evening this room was magically transformed into a family bedroom, as we took down the lavishly hand-embroidered beddings from the deep, huge shelves in the walls and spread them on the floor on a carpet or "killim", only to fold them up the following morning and neatly stack them on the shelves, making sure that the embroidery, which is the proud proof of the skillful feminine fingers of the household, was on open display to the competitive neighbors or friends who might pay us a visit. As you might have already guessed, the whole family slept in this one room. However, during the warm summer, nights were spent on the veranda under the twinkling stars, with our huge mulberry tree overhead gently fanning our faces with a cool, gentle breeze.

In these simple, modestly built homes in Turkey, we *needed* no furniture. We *slept, sat* (on cushions) and *ate* very comfortably on the floor. We *had*, however, a few copper dishes which had been fired and hammered by the blacksmith. The few tiny china cups and saucers that the average family *possessed were* treasured and *were* used only on special occasions such as weddings *and* funerals.

Naomi's Story

We also kept a few specially hand embroidered cushions which *were placed* at the disposal of our guests while they sat on the floor.

Strange as it may seem, a mere clay wall about a foot thick is the only means of separating a home from that of its neighbors on either side, and one long flat "community roof" covered as many as five homes. By the use of a small stepladder suspended from the lower veranda to the roof, one could easily gain access to any of the neighboring homes, which was indeed, God's own curse on humanity in times of the incredibly frequent massacres that the Turks waged on the Armenians.

I may safely say that Saturday in Turkey is the busiest and the most important day of the week for the industrious Armenians. The day begins with the trying task of bread making at the sleepy hour of 4:00 A.M. While the water, which has been painstakingly and patiently drawn from the well in heavy buckets, is being heated in a very large boiler over a smoking bon-fire for the family washing, the bread making commences. I can still visualize my mother and big sister, as they sat on the floor with folded legs, each holding a large heavy board half across their lap, half on the floor, rolling bread dough until it was flattened about a yard wide and as thick as corn flakes. Then father carefully spread these breads, one at a time, over a flat round hot sheet-iron and baked them, turning them over with a long flat stick. Enough bread is made to last a whole week. They are then stacked up in a very large round wooden box, and put away in the storeroom. As the bread is thin and very brittle and crumbles easily, it must first be lightly sprinkled with water and covered with a clean cloth for a few seconds before eating it.

Equally trying and long is the process of washing clothes, which must be done entirely by hand without the aid of a washing machine or even a washboard (such blessing were unknown in Turkey). Even the water for the entire family washing must be heated over a bon-fire, which is continuously smoking, filling the eyes of those around it with blinding, smarting smoke. After each of the three soap washings, the clothes are beaten with a heavy wooden paddle and finally boiled in water into which ashes have been previously added and strained. They are then rinsed in clear water and hung in the sun on the lower veranda.

Next the house is thoroughly and immaculately cleaned. A hurried lunch follows. Then bundling a set of clean clothes for each member of the family—minus men folk, (they go during the evening at special hours)—we hike up to the bathhouse. If a bathhouse in a district different from that in which we live is favored, we willingly go there, covering many miles on foot and then walk back home.

For the benefit of those who might be interested, I shall attempt to briefly describe the interior of one of these Turkish bathhouses called "hamam" and the manner in which we make use of the three hours that are allotted to the bathers.

Entering through the street door, we find ourselves in a large delightfully cool room in the center of which is a beautiful round fountain, where ice cold water continuously flows day and night. The ceiling is domed, and spotted with countless round pieces of thick glass through which light penetrates into the room. The floor is of smooth tile, and the four thick walls around it are of solid cement, lavishly painted with many gaily colored figures and designs—perhaps for the purpose of soothing one's nerves before entering into the hot chambers. Three feet off the floor all along the four walls, is a wide cement platform where we climb up and undress, and wrapping around each of us a large piece of cloth of somewhat carnival colors, step off the platform and hurry into the next compartment.

There we can readily feel the stuffy warmth of the steam that is awaiting us in the next room, and hear the muffled voices of the bathers within. Going through the wringing door, we gasp for a breath of air, as the sudden rush of hot steam quickly envelopes us. For a fraction of a minute we see nothing, but soon the eyes get accustomed to the misty interior, and we find our way to the huge tile platform in the center of the room. The only means of light in the bathing compartments, which are separated from this platform by a space of two yards all around, is through the massive dome above, which is likewise inset with numerous pieces of round glass. The interior of all the compartments is of cement, with the floors of smooth tile of maroon color.

From the two opposite walls of each of the eight bathing rooms that an ordinary bathhouse can boast of, hot water runs for a period of about three hours. As many as eight families are allowed into each room, four at each end, all madly striving to fill their copper buckets with hot water with which to bathe. As the different members of each family are bathed, and their hair cleaned with

Naomi's Story

special 'clay' of greenish color, they are sent onto the large platform for a rest. Some will leisurely take a nap, some will play and still others enjoy with much gusto, the fruits that they have brought along. A second and final bathing usually follows. But for those who are a bit too slow or waste too much idle time on the platform, this right is denied, for at the expiration of three hours the water is shut off and all are obligated to vacate the rooms. Going into the outer room we dressed in our clean clothes, and paying a small fee at the doorway for each member of the family, start for home carrying back with us our soiled clothes and the wet bath towels.

Contrary to the busy Saturdays, our Sundays are spent very quickly and with much reverent respect. We do no work whatsoever, not as much as even sew on a button on a garment in need of it.

As the huge chimes from the high steeples of different churches in various districts clearly ring through the still air, each family dressed in their very best apparel, slowly walk up to their favorite church.

How impressively peaceful and beautiful is the interior of these churches. Hundreds of pleasing scenes from the various Biblical stories are magnificently carved and painted over the old walls and the ceiling, and the massive, gorgeous chandeliers of clear sparkling crystals of white and of varied colors, bedecked with tall, white burning candles, are securely suspended overhead at the end of heavy chains.

It is an undisputed fact that men, women and children alike, will dutifully remove their shoes or sandals before entering into the sacred church, and each humbly kneeling down on the carpeted floor will send a silent prayer before the clear voice of the minister, garbed in a long gorgeously jeweled cape and crown, breaks the hushed silence. The long sermon is followed by a beautiful procession composed of a score of choirmen, all dressed in pure white gowns, and headed by the minister, parade up and down the long aisles, singing various hymns. With a final prayer of thanks to our God, and for his continued blessings upon us, we return to our humble homes.

I must mention here, too, that one of the oldest, the most important and the most endearing customs we Armenian Christians observe is during the Easter time. On Saturday before Easter, and before bedtime, we Armenians cover our hands up to the wrists, and our feet up to the ankles, with henna paste, then wrapping them up with cloth, tie them up tight before retiring for the night. Next day—The Easter Sunday, we uncover our hands and feet, which are now sort of dark reddish-orange color. This is to signify the blood Christ shed when he was crucified and nailed on the cross by his hands and feet. This color lasts for several weeks or so, and will eventually fade away by many washings, and by time.

Such is the simple and devoted life that we Armenians lead in Turkey. Equally simple, but interesting, are the hot summer months that we spend in the vineyards. How childishly happy and thrilled we would all get on the day when father came home with two donkeys, rented for the summer, and packing a few necessities, start off for the vineyards, about half a day's journey. I remember father putting me and my little brother Meenas, each in one of the large hand woven baskets tied on each side of the saddle, while big sister sat on the saddle keeping an eye on me and my brother. Mother rode the other donkey, which had our beddings tied on each side of the saddle. Father and my big brother led the two donkeys on foot, walking all the way to the vineyards.

In the vineyard that we owned we had over a thousand grapevines, producing more than a dozen varieties of delicious grapes. During the three months that we spend in the vineyard we work very hard under the sweltering sun, as all the grapes must be taken care of before they go to waste. From these grapes we make kegs full of rich, dark delicious syrup, hundreds of pounds of meaty raisins, and many, many varieties of toothsome sweetmeats that are unknown to the American people, to say nothing of the gallons of clear sparkling wine that are stored in the cellar. When everything is prepared and packed, the problem of carrying them all to the town is sometimes very grave, as all the trips must be made on donkeys back and forth, sometimes requiring as many as ten days. After all is safely brought home, they are stored away in the storeroom, giving us a secure and satisfied feeling, and making it easier for us to face the long, bitterly cold winter months ahead.

These cold winter days will find us snugly settled in our family den, as we literally imprison ourselves in this room for the entire winter. There are no amusement places such as theatres, dance halls, etc., in Turkey, and all our evenings are spent at home. Our only means of heat is by the use of a small round iron grate, supported by three iron legs standing about six inches off the floor.

Naomi's Story

We manage to keep a handful of coal fire all day by putting fresh pieces of coal from a bucket kept nearby, and gathering around it to keep our hands warm and go on with our work, while the kerosene lamp burning constantly from a shelf above, casting sinister shadows all over the walls. There is mother on one side of the room busy with her spinning and throwing forth such melodious tunes, while the rest of us seated on the floor around the small precious fire, picked sacks of cotton from their shells, and putting them through the cotton-gin, prepare them for spinning. The various skeins of the spun cotton are then dyed into different colors. Then father spent many weeks painstakingly setting these colored skeins in his home-made loom and wove them into attractive afghans from which the family's clothes are made.

It was on such quiet "cotton-shelling" nights that father used to tell us little stories—stories of massacres and blood-sheds that have occurred in Turkey from time to time (before my time) and which our family had been fortunate enough to escape. How these stories of horror thrilled my little heart, and child that I was I wished some day to see such massacres, and be able to talk about them like my father, none of us suspecting once at the time that in less than a year our happy home was to be broken, and the family exiled, along with thousands of other Armenian families, by the long arm of the hideous World War I.

There is one day that stands out so clearly in my mind, as this day marked the beginning of the advancing shadows of the Great War that would eventually touch our happy family. Just before the noon recess (I had been attending the first grade school now for several months) our class was interrupted by a great commotion out in the street below. Curious to know what the excitement and noises were all about, we made a mad rush to the windows and looked down. To our astonishment we witnessed a huge mob of people—Armenians—with their cattle and mules, being driven down the road by scores of Turkish soldiers who were on their horses and swinging their horsewhips wildly, dealing out such stinging blows to the innocent victims in their reach, causing them to issue forth cries of pain and suffering that would curdle the blood in any man's heart—except a Turk's, who has no heart. Some of the people exhausted from endless walking and from lack of food, succumbed on the road dying. The cruel soldiers mercilessly ran their horses over these unfortunates and left them there dying a slow death. Without any explanation to us bewildered children the teacher dismissed us for the rest of the day.

Upon reaching the street where our house was located, I was surprised to see that all the women in the neighborhood had gathered there near the road, watching the unfortunate Armenians and their cattle go by. Spying my mother in the crowd, I ran to her and taking hold of her apron, clung to her. She encircled a loving arm around my shoulders and pressed me close to her. But she was crying. Everybody around me was crying. Their faces uplifted toward the sky, they murmured queer words to themselves, meanwhile beating their chests with their fists. When we returned home, mother went quietly to a corner, and kneeling down began to pray. It seemed as though the happy atmosphere about our home had suddenly changed into silent gloom.

Still greatly mystified at the cause of this sudden change, I went to bed. But I heard my father and mother talking, talking about the big mob of people we had seen going through our town. Father was saying that those people were all Armenians living in Armenia when the Turks were driving them into exile, where they would all be massacred, or perished by hunger. Before very long he said the Turks would start exiling all the Armenians living in Turkey, which would include us. I heard them mention the year 1916.

As time went on, little riots broke out in various sections of town, and many arrests of innocent Armenians were made. Twice my big brother was arrested on his way home, by the Turks, and word was sent to us to bail him out. So unreasonably high were these bails that it would take us weeks to obtain the sufficient amount, knowing all the time that my brother, together with many other innocent prisoners, were going through many physical tortures administered to them by their barbaric jailers.

Finally, in the wake of 1917, the dreadful exiling nosed its way into Marash, Turkey. The Mohammedans lost no time in spreading destruction, disaster and death in every direction, sparing no feeling whatsoever. Already scores of families had been turned out of their homes and were on their way to exile—to death. DEATH, whether it be by starvation, by perishing in the hot doomed desert, or by the sharp blow of a sword or of a bayonet dealt by a Turk who feels he is perfectly justified in whatever harm he does to a 'Christian dog'; as they call Armenians.

Naomi's Story

As they neared our district, my father's fears and sorrows increased, for he knew that we would be among the unfortunates to be exiled, to be slaughtered. Then suddenly his face brightened. Why not close the house and move into a different district until things quieted down in our section? This didn't seem a bad idea. So we packed up a few necessities and moved to the opposite side of town, to live with one of my aunts who had unsparingly accumulated a large family of twelve healthy children. This family composed of the goodly sum of fourteen members, and ours of the modest eight, strived to live the best we could in their little four room house for about two months.

Once during our stay here, father and a couple of his friends got the foolish idea into their heads that they wanted to go to the vineyards and work around for a few days, as the vines needed some timely attention. Instantly mother began to plead with them and begged them to give up this crazy notion. But, no! Once their minds were made up nobody could persuade them to stay. So at the break of dawn one morning, they started out. Mother, meanwhile, was sick over the whole thing. We felt certain something dreadful would befall them. I can still see how she prayed and cried all morning.

Then to our surprise, around noon the same day, father came back, pale as a ghost, his forehand covered with tiny beads of perspiration. He rushed in as an insane man and locked the door after him. When he finally recovered his breath and voice, raspingly he told us that they had hardly reached the city limits, when they saw four Armenian men lying dead on the road—beheaded and robbed of their meager valuables, by the Turks. Going on a mile or two further, he said they saw one more victim, apparently also going to the vineyards, but suffered the same fate the others had. It was too much he said. They lost their nerve and turning back, hurried toward home thinking only of their lives.

People all around were certainly acting queer lately. Almost every day men and women alike would go up to the churches off the schedule and pray for hours. They would wrap themselves in old carpets and rags and put ashes on their heads, and rocking back and forth on their knees, would cry and pray. Some of them would remain there all night waiting to hear God answer their prayers and save them from the Turks. I just couldn't figure out what it was all about. What was war anyway?

Two months having elapsed since we moved into my aunt's place, father thought perhaps we could now go back to our home. Surely exiling in that part of the town must be over by now. Getting our family and the few belongings together, but still feeling a bit skeptical about our safety, we returned to our happy home.

Taking a brief inventory of our neighborhood we found that all the families had been exiled, all but two who were so poor and lived in such miserably small shacks that the Turks hadn't bothered to go near them. They could kill them anytime.

How quiet and deserted the homes and street were. There was no more happy childish laughter to fill the sky. The ceaseless buzz of the flies only added weight to the distressing atmosphere. The many gaily colored flowers and plants raised so painstakingly in each home had dried down to their roots. Where were their proud owners? Where were those once happy people and their children now? Perhaps some of them were already dead. How lucky it was that our family had escaped their fate. But had we? Who can escape the far-reaching hand of 'destiny'? Our doom was but a few days away had we only realized it then.

It all started on a beautiful June day in 1917. We had just returned home from the Turkish public bathhouse and were on the lower veranda leisurely passing the time while big sister was busy preparing dinner. Mother was sitting under the huge mulberry tree knitting a wool sweater for me, wool that she herself had carded and spun. Then quietly the door opened and there stood father, his head bowed and big drops of tears running down his cheeks. In his hand he held a small piece of paper. Mother looked at my father, looked at the paper in his hand, turned white and fainted. How this incident lives vividly in my memory. That little bit of paper spelled our doom. It was our notice of exile.

The 'generous' Turks had allowed us one week in which to get ready and depart. We had an option, however. We could denounce our religion and accept Mohammedans, that is, go out and fight against our own people and intermarry our boys and girls with the Turks. An uncle, or should I say my mother's uncle had already become a Turk months before and was doing his share of leaving a trail of destruction everywhere he went—cold blooded that he was. The yellow scoundrel! But, he was safe, he didn't have to be exiled. He figured he had gotten the best of the bargain. Mother thought of him and shivered. She and her family would

Naomi's Story

never denounce Christ she said. We would go to exile and suffer as God willed it.

The first thing Father did was to go out and buy a large canvas tent. Oh what fun we would have sleeping in that tent. I was completely overjoyed, anxious for the day of departure and thinking only of the new lands we would see. (Ah, the blessed innocence of childhood that knows neither tragedy nor sorrow). Next father auctioned the bedding, and the one set of beautiful silverware which was the family pride and which was used only in honor of company—we had wooden spoons for our daily use—the gunny sacks full of staples, in order to have some ready cash on hand. You see, we had to either sell our things or leave them behind, as we could take with us only what we could carry on our backs.

Mother meanwhile, had been doing some fast thinking. She knew that exile held but one definite fate for us—death! Why should the whole family, eight members, be wiped off completely from the face of the earth? Why not take a chance and leave at least one member behind to represent the doomed family? She decided my sixteen-year-old sister was best suited for the purpose. We had an old family friend, an Armenian dentist. He and his family had been exempt from exile on condition that he render free dental service to any Turk who might be in need of it, to which he, the dentist, had willingly agreed. Knowing this, mother asked him if she could leave my sister in his care. Certainly—he was only too glad to honor my mother's wishes.

When mother hopefully told her plan to my sister, it was like throwing a bomb into the fire. Instantly sister broke into hysterics. She would not, she said, POSITIVELY WOULD NOT separate from the family. She said she would go with us and die with us. Neither of my parents could reason with her. At night she would have nightmares of being left behind and would shrilly cry out "don't leave me, don't leave me" and would frantically try to tear up the bed covers. In hopeless despair mother dismissed the idea of leaving her behind.

We now had just two days left before that dreadful day when we would be driven away, like horses and cattle going into slaughter. Mother was still determined to leave someone behind. Putting on her shawl and taking hold of my chubby little arm, she told me we were going out for a walk. Surprised at this sudden treat, I trotted along kicking the pebbles and the little rocks off the dirt road with my bare feet and trying to keep up with mother's big steps.

What a long walk this was! I was getting awful tired. I asked my mother where we were going. She only tightened her grip on my hand and without uttering a word kept going straight on. Strange! Would we never stop. There were hardly any homes around us now. Still we continued further on.

Then suddenly we came near a very large building, the biggest I'd ever seem, which had a high wall all around it. I could now hear a lot of voices, voices of girls coming from the building. In a moment I realized where mother was taking me—the orphanage! I stiffened. It seemed as though my feet had suddenly rooted fast to the ground. I could not go on a step further. Feeling the tension of my body, mother instantly grasped my arm and practically dragged me on the street toward the orphanage, turning a deaf ear to my frantic cries. Did she mean that she was going to leave me in the orphanage while the rest of the family went to exile? Why, that couldn't be! My mother wouldn't do that. But here we were already at the huge steel door and she was knocking with the old iron knocker.

My wild cries had evidently attracted quite an attention within, for as the great door slowly began to swing open, I was obliged to see about sixty girls all in uniforms, staring at me. Then a gray haired gentle looking woman came to the door and right away my mother began to beg her to please take me in as our family was about to be exiled. I burst into fresh cries and tried to run away. But mother was holding me tight, so tight that it hurt my wrist. The kind woman looked at me pityingly and told my mother that she couldn't possibly admit me as she already had over three hundred orphans to feed and look after. Mother's grip relaxed and I ran down the street happy that I didn't have to stay in the orphanage. But, Mother wasn't coming. She was still talking with that lady. I sat down on the road and waited. Perhaps the merciful hand of fate was guarding over me and prompted me to leave my mother just then, for had I remained there and heard the conversation, my life would have been a different one now, or perhaps I wouldn't have lived to tell the story.

That evening after supper mother told me that she was going to let me live with our dentist friend and his family instead of my sister because she loved me best. She said I would have many pretty dresses, lots of nice things to eat and go to school. Being a child and easily influenced, my mind was readily made up. I didn't want to go to exile and get killed anyway.

Early the following morning, Saturday, the day of exile—I woke to see Mother sitting on the floor beside my bed, softly crying and lovingly stroking my hair. She bent over and kissed my forehead, her hot tears falling on my face. I had never seen Mother do that before. It was rather strange that she should give me such a morning greeting. Before I could inquire as to her odd actions she gently gathered me in her arms and carried me to breakfast, our last family breakfast in our happy home. In a few hours we would all be driven away. None of us could eat anything. My parents and my oldest sister and brother were all crying as if someone had suddenly died. Feeling the depressing gloom about me I began to cry too.

By ten o'clock Father had carried down the few necessary articles that they intended to take with them, such as blankets, clothes and several sacks of food. They couldn't take much of a load as whatever they took with them had to be carried on their backs.

A few Turkish women had already come to our house, invading the rooms and taking an inventory of what we were leaving behind. It was now a matter of hours when they would move in and comfortably establish themselves in our home. The very presence of them, their sneering looks and insulting remarks almost drove me insane. Yet we could not say anything to them but sit on the street in front of the door and await the fatal order to go. Father drew a bucket of water from the well from which we all drank to our hearts content. each one inwardly wondering with sickening despair when we would taste water again.

My aunt had come to take me away. I was to stay with her over the weekend and on Monday morning she was to take me to my new home, our dentist friend's home. Suddenly an idea flashed in my mind. Why couldn't I take my blue eyed, golden haired, three-year-old sister with me? I loved her and it would be nice if we grew up together. While mother was talking to my aunt I managed to lift my sister under the arms and carried her to the next street, intending to pick her up as Auntie and I passed by. But leaving her thus by herself worried me because I feared some Turk might harm her, and brought her back. I repeated this three times, uncertain of what was best to do. On my fourth trip mother saw me in the act and asked me where I was taking sister. When I told her she scolded me severely and said I would only cause her trouble by doing that because, she explained, the Turks wouldn't miss just one, but if two or three members were left behind, they would notice the sudden change in the family's size and cause her trouble and then even I couldn't stay. So my little idea went 'puff'.

Presently my aunt walked over to me and handed me an orange and some sweets, and taking hold of my hand she started walking toward the end of the street and kept going down the next and the next. I was busy eating my orange and didn't realize we were drifting away from home. We walked and walked and walked. But I didn't mind it. I was thoroughly enjoying my orange and candy, unaware of the ghastly tragedy that was hanging over my head that very moment.

The next thing I knew we had reached her home. As we stepped inside the street door, my aunt gave a great sigh, and closing the door after us, put on the heavy bolt. At the same time, something snapped inside of me, as if bringing me out of a daze. Suddenly I realized that I was away from my family, that I would never see them again. A sickening realization told me that I had lost them forever, seven of them. A chill went through me. How quickly the dreadful thing had happened. Why, I hadn't even said goodbye to my family. Wildly running to the door I tried to open it, but couldn't even budge the heavy iron bolt. Helpless and growing hysterical, I begged my aunt to take me back to my people before it was too late. But, ignoring me entirely, she went on with her work. It had been part of the plan to get me away before the hour of exile to prevent any possible outburst on my part at the last moment, thus ruining their whole plan.

The whole thing seemed so incredible. I never knew before that it was ever possible for anyone to be so miserable. It seemed as though the whole weight of the world had suddenly fallen upon my young shoulders. It is absolutely impossible for me to express in mere words, the unfathomable loneliness that overcame me. Only the person who had the misfortune of going through such a heart rendering, utterly wrenching experience can justly sympathize with my feelings at this hour of darkness. Cry? Yes indeed! I cried my very heart out, cried until no more tears would come. But all the bitter tears I shed brought me no relief, instead they added assurance to the fact that I had become an orphan. How the hours of that Saturday afternoon stretched every minute cruelly repeating the fact over and over in my mind that I would never see my family again, that I was now a true orphan. I think this day was the most bitter day of my life. Although I was only seven years of age at the time, the tragedy left such a deep wound in my heart that I've lived through it all a million times during the years that followed, each day of the numbering years cutting still deeper into my broken heart.

Somehow, I survived through the weekend. Then came Monday morning. After a hurried breakfast my aunt and I started out, supposedly headed for my new home. Still nursing my heavy loss, my eyes were full of tears, my mind full of thoughts of my family, wondering where they were now. We kept going, going. I didn't know what direction, and I didn't care.

After a period of what seemed to me to be ages, I was amazed to discover that we had come to the familiar sight of the huge building with the high wall around it. I could now plainly hear the voices of the girls. Still we advanced toward the orphanage. Surely there must be a misunderstanding somewhere. Before I realized it, we reached the immense iron door. My aunt knocked, the door swung open, she pushed me in, and the door closed tight again. No words were exchanged. Evidently I was expected here at this hour of the day.

The fact that I was actually in the orphanage made no sense. What about the friend with whom I was to live? This must be a dream, a hideous nightmare. Yet already over a hundred girls had gathered around me, all staring at me, and whispering to each other. The shock, the disappointment of it all was too much for me. I collapsed to the ground crying my heart out.

Two girls in uniforms picked me up and carried me to the orphanage's bathhouse. Scrubbing me from head to toe they clothed me in the traditional orphan's uniform and presented me to the head of the orphanage—the same lady who only four days ago had talked with my mother and said she didn't want me. In a moment it flashed to my mind that I had been the victim of some cruel trick. The sickening realization that slowly crept to my heart was some time later confirmed by my aunt who admitted that she had only carried out my mother's wishes. Now here I was just another one of the three hundred orphans. This was to be my new home for God knows how long.

The first few months were sheer torture to me. I was so lonely and missed my family so, that every little thought of them would force the tears to my eyes. At night I would dream about them and cry out in my sleep, disturbing the room full of girls, until someone would shout at me to shut up and that I would get use to being an orphan as they all had. But somehow I just couldn't get use to it. My loss seemed heavier than anyone's around me. In losing my family I lost my heart. My very life seemed to have oozed away.

As time went on I became more and more convinced that I could not get used to the orphanage. I felt like a caged bird. How I longed to get outside those thick walls and be free. This secret desire of mine increased daily until one day my chance to escape was almost realized. I had been on the lookout for a clear getaway, and so at the first chance I made my exit through the cellar door—out into the wide deserted street.

I ran for a block then stopped dead short. Now that I was out I didn't know what to do with my newly acquired freedom. I dared not go too far lest I might encounter a Turk who might take a sudden fancy to stone me or even kill me. My uniform betrayed me. As I stood there wondering what to do, someone had spied me from the orphanage and given the alarm. The next moment I was being chased and cornered by four of the 'big sisters' who brought me safely back. Besides the failure of my long planned scheme, I had to undergo a punishment. During the supper hour that evening I was obliged to remain standing and to bear the stare of three hundred pair of eyes focused on me in shame. And to top it all, I was deprived of my supper.

Gradually I began to take interest in things around me. First of all I must take in hand the great task of learning the names of all the girls if I was to live with them. That required time. Then there was the everlasting daily routine, during which every hour of the day was accounted for.

The best part of the days were spent in the school, a building of its own, also within the huge walls surrounding the entire orphanage. Because this orphanage was under German supervision at the time, most of our subjects were in German language. However, twice a week our Armenian teachers were permitted to give us lessons in writing and reading Armenian and Turkish. But everyday from 8 o'clock in the morning until 4 o'clock in the afternoon

Naomi's Story

(the school hours) we were obliged to speak only German and avoid both the Armenian and the Turkish languages. Anyone failing to obey this simple rule suffered a punishment.

It is with bitter contempt and hate that I recall to my mind the undying friendship of the Germans to the Turks. To prove their loyalty to the Mohammedans, the Germans compelled us orphans, twice a month, to salute the Turkish flag and to sign to it, while the Turkish officials witnessed the ceremony with fiendish delight. They forbade us to ever mention the name of our own flag. Yes, the Germans were rewarded for their 'faithfulness' as they were warned and given a chance to leave the town just before the great massacre of 1920.

At the age of ten, three years after I entered the orphanage I could speak, read and write Armenian, German and Turkish. In all of my classes I was voted the most brilliant student and received an award at the end of each school year during the program presented in the orphanage. One year I was given an Armenian-Turkish Bible with my teacher's signature, which I brought to America and which I still cherish to this day.

During these three years, I had also earned for myself the title of being the best all around, the most popular girl among the entire three hundred orphans. Allow me, dear reader, to mention an incident of which I am very proud, even to this day.

One day a handsome red wool sweater, along with a letter, arrived from Germany addressed to the German Missionary in charge of our orphanage. The letter requested that the sweater be given to the most deserving girl. During supper that evening the Missionary came down and holding the letter in one hand and the sweater in the other, asked us who should get it. In a moment there was an uproar of voices all calling my name. "Give it to Naomi Kalemjian, give it to Naomi Kalemjian." (Bless their hearts). Their shouts still seem to ring in my ears. I got the sweater and was allowed to wear it, thus distinguishing me from the rest of the girls, as all the others wore the usual navy blue uniforms (gingham dresses).

I was also granted special favors now and then. On one occasion, a Sunday in November, 1919, I went to see my younger aunt, sister to the aunt who brought me to the orphanage, and of whom I was quite fond. Her husband was a baker. They had two sons, ages six and eight years old. I had gone to visit this aunt on every possible chance, but on this here particular day something seemed to be on her mind. Just before I left her home to return to the orphanage she broke down with the astounding news that my mother had a sister who had gone to America long before I was born. This came to me as a thunderbolt from a clear sky. Mother had never mentioned this sister of hers to us. Then she suggested that we write to this aunt in America and inform her of my family's fate, and of my being in the orphanage. Of course nothing might come out of it. We'd be taking a chance in a million, as at that time all the mail going out of Turkey was censored, thus being opened at the Turkish post office and their contents read. If a letter were written in a language that the Turks couldn't read, it was immediately destroyed. If written in Turkish, they would read it and either send it through or destroy it, depending on the contents. Thus we would be taking a great chance, but it would hurt nobody. My aunt wrote the letter and mailed it. With new hopes for the future and with a light heart I returned to the orphanage, unaware of the fact that I had visited my aunt and her family for the last time.

Just about two months after this visit all the Germans in charge of our orphanage and of the other orphanages, left town to return to Germany. There had been some innocent rumors that in the near future American Missionaries were to resume the responsibility of caring for the orphans. So naturally we gave no more thought to their sudden departure. The daily routine went on as usual. Schools continued without interruption.

Slowly, the bitter month of December gave way to the even colder month of January 1920, the month during which I experienced such horrible events that to this day they have been nothing less than the most hideous nightmares a human being could possibly experience. It all started without warning, on a quiet happy holiday, the day on which we Christians were observing the Christmas Day (our Christmas is celebrated during the first week in January).

About 4:00 o'clock in the afternoon a few of my close friends and I had left the large stuffy room where over sixty girls were huddled around a small portable stove to keep warm, and stepped out to the open veranda to admire the hundreds of beautiful trees and roofs heavily laden with spotless snow. As we leaned on the railing and leisurely looked over the white city, we let our imagination run astray and fancied a happy little group of Christians gathered around a cheery fire under each Armenian roof, exchanging friendly visits, discussing the special Christmas ceremonies they had enjoyed, and piece-mealing various delicious sweetmeats. We closed our eyes and imagined we were there with them, when presto, we were rudely started from our daydreams by the shrill bark of a rifle fired at close range, a bullet whizzing close overhead. Before we could gather our senses here came another shot, and another. In a moment the big gong sent its pealing chimes through the orphanage and immediately the three hundred and ten orphans fell in line in their accustomed places, then quickly began pouring into the huge dining room, which was built almost under ground. But already we could hear people running wildly up and down in the streets outside the high walls, their horrified shrieks and cries filling the sky with "it has come—it has come—the massacre." "Allah, have mercy on us." Indeed it didn't take long to realize that we poor Christians were once more at the mercy of the cold blooded Turks, like a flock of helpless sheep left to the mercy of a pack of hungry wolves. The mere fact that World War I had been over for more than two years didn't mean a thing to the heartless Mohammedans. They were hungry for more Christian blood and they chose this Christmas Day, knowing that the majority of the Armenians were away from their home. Already many homes were going up in flames. Even the orphanages were left unprotected at this dreadful time. Surely the Germans must have known of this impending peril as they were and always have been, in eternal friendly terms with the Turks. Informed beforehand, they had thus left the country in a hurry lest they may witness the horrors of the bloody massacre!

    I shall never, in all the years to come, forget that first dreadful night we spent in the dining room. Not daring to go up to the sleeping chambers or to even show a light in any of the other rooms, we were cooped up in this one large room, sitting on the bare floor and everybody crying out in terror. Little children of four or five years of age frightened at the continuous shots, yelled at the top of their lungs, while we girls of but a few years their senior played sisters to them and vainly attempted to pacify them, although we ourselves were simply frantic with ever-increasing fright. Super time came and they handed to each of us a chunk of bread and a piece of cheese. But who could eat a bite while wholesale human slaughtering was in full swing just outside the walls and our lives only a matter of a few short hours, as we then presumed. Bedtime arrived and although rooms full of beds neatly arranged in long rows in the chambers above awaited us, we remained where we were.

The burdened hours of the night slowly ticked on, each hour claiming a heavy toll of innocent lives. Then came the dawn. Still the shooting and the burning of homes continued unmercifully. Late in the afternoon we saw from where we were, our leading Christian church going up in flames. It burned for many, many, long hours, its twisting black smoke rising higher and higher into the dark skies, as if appealing for the mercies of the God Almighty above who seemed to have turned against all mankind. Later I learned, much to my grievance, that over five hundred Armenians had fled to this church for shelter, among them one of my cousins and her grandmother. The Turks had cunningly allowed these poor victims to go to the church, and when the place was full to its capacity, had locked all the doors and windows, and pouring barrels of kerosene oil all around, set fire to it, shooting down anyone who frantically attempted to escape.

Day after day stretched on, but still the slaughtering continued. Being unable to secure fresh food supplies for the orphanage, and economizing on the staples we already had stored away, our meals were cut down to two a day, each meal being just enough to keep the body and soul together. Scores of younger children became ill due to under-nourishment and to fright. Each day and night a group of Turks vainly tried to break their way into our orphanage and satisfy their fiendish blood-thirst. But the merciful hand of God in the form of a few French soldiers kept guard over us, and their attempts proved futile.

Eight such horrible long days, days of hell, we experienced. On the morning of the ninth day all shooting and a proclamation was issued throughout the city, stating that all the roads would be open until 9:00 o'clock that night for the surviving Armenians to leave the town unmolested, and that at this affixed hour they, the Turks, would make a house to house raid, killing any and all Armenians they found, then burning their homes. A few hours later the miserable people began to crawl out of their hiding places. Shaking with fright for fear the cheating Turks might shoot them down in the back and stumbling over the countless dead bodies scattered all over the streets, the much abused Christians gathered into large groups in various districts to leave town simultaneously.

Naomi's Story

Such a gathering was materializing at a place just two blocks from the orphanage. Despite the freezing temperature and the ever increasing snow and the blizzard, many of the older girls left the orphanage to join the mob. Even the supervisor, whom we had been in the habit of calling 'mother' joined them, leaving us prey to any army of blood-drinking Turks that would be swarming in that night. That settled everything for me. I would join the crowd outside and go where they go. Putting on my worn out sandals and slipping into the red wool sweater that had once been presented with such high honors to me, I passed through the huge steel door, out into the shivering and morbid world—ice and snow.

I struggled on for a block or so. The bitter cold had already numbed my hands and feet, but I went on. Finally I reached the crowd, and seeing two of the girls from the orphanage, went over to them. But, they turned away, paying no attention to me. Nobody paid any attention to anybody. It was a case of everyone for himself. Presently the crowd began to move on. I started too, but, soon discovered that I could not keep pace with them. I lingered behind, and eventually lost all sight of them.

There I stood, a child of ten years, alone, cold and hungry, bareheaded, in the midst of a blizzard. My aching hands and feet were becoming positively unbearable with pain. I felt certain I would freeze to death within a few hours. Oh well, as long as I was doomed to die what difference did it make whether I froze to death, or died from the flow of a Turk's sword. It was God's will. Somehow through that awful, blinding blizzard, I threaded my way back to the orphanage, falling to my knees in the blinding snow and wind, and after much knocking and calling my name in an attempt to convince them that I was not an outsider, and belonged there, the huge door finally opened just enough for me to squeeze in. Oh, God! How good it was to be back inside, with all these little children.

The fateful evening arrived. The ninth day of the bloody massacre. It would soon be over. Slowly the big clock on the wall chimed the hour of disaster and destruction—9:00 o'clock. We all sat up tense, rigid, waiting, waiting, for the deafening roar of the guns, waiting for the sharp sword of the Turks to fall on our necks to chop off our heads. We were just helpless children. We waited in utter misery and fright. But the peaceful silence of the night remained unbroken. 9:00 o'clock ticked its way to 10:00 o'clock, to

11:00 o'clock, to midnight—still nothing happened. We all sat in the dark (about 300 orphans) and waited. Little kids began to cry. Others tried to "hush" them to be quiet. We were all hungry, cold and frightened. We all sat in the dark, waiting, waiting. It was strange. Was this another trick of the deceitful Mohammedans or had they run out of ammunition? Was it possible that they had at last satisfied their thirst for blood and had gone home to purr with fiendish satisfaction and glee? The hours ticked by peacefully. Wondering when the blessed silence would be disturbed by the roar of the guns. We sat up all night waiting, every minute torturing us with sickening suspense.

The next morning found the city in no worse condition than it had been the previous day. The ugly massacre had ceased as suddenly as it had started. Although there was no more shooting or burning of homes, it was several days before the remaining people, who were poor and wretched indeed, felt safe enough to venture out of their homes or hiding places.

Exactly a week after the massacre had stopped, my uncle who had somehow miraculously escaped unharmed, came to the orphanage to see me, a wild look in his eyes. He stayed only five minutes, but what he told me during those five minutes left such a tragic blotch in my memory that the course of years can never erase. Having been away from his home and family at the time of the sudden outbreak of the massacre, he said he was forced to remain where he was. But as soon as the slaughtering had stopped, he had rushed home to his wife and two sons, rushed home to find them all dead—beheaded, and, his home completely in ruins. Before I could make any sense to his words he was gone. I have never seen him or heard of him to this day. Cold and shuddering from the shock, I sat down and thought of the last visit I had spent with my aunt about three months ago, the visit during which she had written that letter to America.

Gradually the weeks grew into months and the long winter months gave way to the more pleasant and hopeful spring. With the coming of spring also came the merciful missionaries from America. It seemed as though these good Americans spread sunshine everywhere they went. I cannot praise enough the wonderful things they were doing daily for the poor surviving Christians. They gave them warm clothes that had been collected in America and sent over by the Red Cross and the Near East Relief workers.

Naomi's Story

They gave free medical aid to anyone who needed it, which numbered into the hundreds. Even when the destructive 'cholera' found its way to our city during the summer sending hundreds upon hundreds to bed and to their grave, these angels of mercy worked unceasingly day and night saving what lives they could. Yes the 'cholera' even visited our orphanage taking with it the lives of four small children. I suffered with it for some time too, but the good lord didn't want me just yet, and in due time I regained my health and strength.

An American missionary by the name of Miss A.E. Mather assumed complete charge of our orphanage and with the assistance of the new supervisor, whom she had engaged, soon established new law and order. True, many of the girls had left the orphanage hoping to escape the massacre on the ninth day of the massacre, but they were replace by two-fold, as the cruel massacre had orphaned hundreds of children whom Miss Mather had rounded up and brought to our orphanage. There were now about five hundred girls to be taken care of. The supervisor set new daily rules for us to follow and gave each girl a new number to be put on every single article she possessed. Mine was #184. Gradually things went back to normal.

In due time Miss Mather opened our schools and employed new teachers to carry on the classes. Instead of German, we were now to study the American language. But our teachers were all Armenians and didn't know a word of English. Miss Mather bravely understood the task of giving these teachers English lessons daily, and they in turn taught us what they learned. It took us weeks to master just the alphabet. It was slow progress, but someday we'd be able to speak this wonderful language.

Having finished in four years, the seven grades in the orphanage, in September 1921, I entered the eighth grade in a different school just three blocks away. I had been attending this school for about six weeks when one day as I came to the orphanage for lunch I found a group of my friends anxiously waiting for me. They informed me that an American nurse, who had just recently come to our city, had come to the orphanage looking for me. Looking for Naomi Kalemjian! I trembled at the news. What could this mean? Excited and swarmed by curious girls all around me, I went to lunch. The supervisor kindly promised to take me to this nurse after school.

Thrills of excitement raced up and down my back all afternoon. And my heart—how fast and loud it was beating. Would 4:00 o'clock ever come? Yes, it did, and as if in a dream I found myself back in the orphanage and later accompanied by the supervisor, going to see the American nurse who was the medium of all my excitement.

Upon reaching our destination we were received by a stately built gray haired and very gentle woman who introduced herself as Miss Ganaway. Through an interpreter Miss Ganaway calmly informed me that she had come from Seattle in America, where I had an aunt living. This aunt had received the letter my aunt and I had sent from Turkey almost two years ago and was very anxious to locate me. Being a dear friend of hers, Miss Ganaway had promised to personally search for me and write to my aunt who, upon hearing from me, would send enough money for me to go to America. My heart skipped a beat. I stood there, numb to the core, staring at the woman before me. It seemed so incredible and yet so miraculous, that this letter, our one chance in a million, had reached America. The idea had been only a passing fancy at the time. The mere thought of going to America, the magic country of the world, or even leaving Turkey for another land, had been beyond my wildest dreams! Yet Miss Ganaway was assuring me that such a thing was quite possible, thus staggering my wildest imaginations. With great satisfaction she requested me to write a letter and give it to her so she could forward it to my aunt under American seal.

The letter was duly sent to America and during the months of anxious waiting that followed, I literally lived in a daze floating in the clouds. I could not keep my mind on my schoolwork. Day and night I imagined I was going to America, imagined the long and adventurous journey that lay ahead, imagined what America and her people would be like, imagined———.

At last, early in December 1921 Miss Ganaway proudly informed me that the money for my journey had arrived from my aunt, and that as soon as she and Miss Mather could obtain a passport for me, I would start for America. My knees weakened, and tears, tears of joy, filled my eyes. For the first time in my life words had deserted me. I could not even say thank you. There are times when mere words are inadequate to express ones extreme sorrow or joy. I reached over and kissed Miss Ganaway's right hand then ran to a lonely corner and softly cried, cried because I was happy beyond feeling.

On January 12, 1922—exactly two years after the massacre—I started on my adventurous journey of eleven thousand miles to America. What thrills and mysteries were in store for me! Why, I had never gone so far as the city limits (except to the vineyards) before, and here I was starting on a journey half way around the world, at the age of twelve. The mere thought of it shook my very soul, my very being!

Miss Mather having expired her term in Turkey was to leave for America the same day as I did. It so happened that about a hundred Armenian families, who of their own free will, were fleeing from Turkey lest another massacre should break before long, were also leaving on this day, with the hope of having Miss Mather as a sort of guard over them against the Turks until they were out of the Turkish domain.

Around noon we took off. Seated, somewhat unsecuredly, on the brown saddle of my rented mule, I surveyed the sea of people and mules so steadily moving ahead. I turned and took one last glance at the city that had offered me no happiness, but instead had cruelly robbed me of my family and of my relatives. It was truly a city of sorrow and bloodshed and curse. Again tears swelled my eyes and a shudder ran through me. I turned my back to the city and with a sigh, wrapped my blanket tightly around me. With a quivering, yet determined chin lifted high and eyes fixed straight ahead on the far horizon, I started on my long journey with fond hopes for a new and happier life, in America.

Five hours later we came to a shaky old wooden bridge, stretched across a furiously roaring river below, which we had to cross. Part of the crowd had already reached the opposite side but I was still on the bridge with half a dozen mules and their riders following behind in a line, when we were startled by the loud report of a rifle close by. The unexpected shot seemed to craze my mule, which started on a wild gallop. At the sudden jerk, my large bag of food containing a few loaves of bread, hunks of cheese, walnuts and raisins, which was hanging from the side of the saddle, went over the bridge, down into the river and was swallowed by the angry waters. Hanging on to the saddle for dear life and screaming, I reached the secure ground, with the others following close behind.

No sooner had we left the bridge, when we were all surrounded by forty Turkish bandits, all masked and armed with rifles and wicked swords. Perhaps they were bidding us farewell. At any rate they ordered us all to get off the mules and unpack everything. Spreading a blanket on the frozen ground, they demanded that 300 liras (about $1500.00) be thrown on it otherwise they would massacre us all. This was an unheard of sum and they knew it. It would give them a very good excuse to butcher us all. We lost all hopes and began to pray God for his mercies, to spare us from these heartless barbarians.

About thirty of the bandits were going from person to person taking any and all valuables or money they could find on them and throwing it all on the blanket, while three others were joyfully engaged taking runs at horse whipping a girl of sixteen years of age just for the sheer amusement. Little children were crying out in terror and trying to hide in their mother's arms. Commotion and excitement surrounded us.

A few of the Turks went over to Miss Mather and demanded that she open her trunk which was filled with priceless handmade American laces and embroidery and countless little souvenirs that she was bringing to America. Naturally she declined. Now, the Turks don't know what it is to have anyone disobey them. Much surprised at her cool refusal, two of them leveled their guns on her ribs and said that unless she opened her trunk they would kill her. Amused at their ignorance, Miss Mather stood erect and plainly said, "Why, you wouldn't dare kill me. I am an American, and I still refuse to open my trunk." Furious with anger, the bandits walked over to the trunk, smashed it open, took what they wanted and dumping the rest of the ground, trampled them into the mud. Frightened beyond feeling and not knowing what to expect next, I sat down and cried and wished I had never left the orphanage.

Two hours later, the bandits told us to pack and continue on our way. Being many miles away from the travelers' inn, people all around hurriedly got on their mules and went off. This was another case of everyone for himself. Although I didn't know the first thing about saddling a mule and couldn't even get on one, nobody paid the slightest attention to me. I stood there wondering how when dear old Miss Mather came to my rescue. Precariously perched on my mule, I mingled with the few remaining families

Naomi's Story

and we started out in a vast empty countryside. It was now pitch dark and very cold.

Before we had gone a mile, I noticed that my mule was limping. He seemed to slow down every step and I was already losing sight and sound of the crowd rushing on ahead. Frantically I tried to urge the beast to speed up when, lo and behold, the forlorn animal stumbled on a rock and lay flat on the road then rolled into a shallow ditch throwing me completely off the saddle. Try as I did I couldn't make him get up. I was stupefied. What would happen to me now? Sitting there all alone on the road, with no building or even a tree in sight, I began to cry and wished I would die or freeze to death on the spot before I suffered any more. I could still hear the rifle shots of the bandits in the far distance as they wildly fired into the sky, as they are apt to do so for mere sport, frightening every living soul that happens to be in their way. I shuddered at the thought—fear numbing my very heart.

Half an hour passed. Hello—someone was approaching in my direction. Was it possible that my suffering was damaging my mental capacity causing me to hear sounds that weren't there at all, or was I really—Yes, I could plainly hear horse's hoofs on the frozen road. I sat there stiffly, open mouthed and simply petrified with fear. I could not move a muscle. The sound came nearer and nearer. Cold sweat began to run down my face. This was no imagination. Now I could hear two persons talking, two familiar voices. To my amazement, I perceived Miss Mather and her interpreter standing before me. A relieved feeling of relaxation came over me. I had taken it for granted they had gone with the crowd, but evidently they had lingered back making sure that no one was left behind. At any rate, I must have represented an object of amusement, for Miss Mather took one look at me miserably sitting on the road by the mule, and laughed heartily. Then helping me out of my sad state, we hurried toward the inn.

Early the next morning we resumed our journey. We crossed many hills and valleys and it was rough going, but nothing extraordinary took place. Constantly Miss Mather kept a guarding eye on me and the other girl from the same orphanage (about ten years old and who, I think, was also going to America). This girl and I could never keep up with the rest of the crowd, having had no experience in traveling on mules, so when late in the evening we entered a small village, we found the inn filled to its utmost capacity and thus were obliged to remain outside. Miss Mather also shared our fate.

Presently the chief of the village, who was an Arab but who could also speak Turkish, came and generously offered his humble shack to Miss Mather for the night. When she asked if she could take us girls too, the chief said no, that we were only Armenians and that the stable was good enough for us. We could sleep either there or out in the cold. Miss Mather refused his offer saying that she couldn't leave us by ourselves. They argued, but at the end, Miss Mather, her interpreter the other girl from the same orphanage and myself, spent the night in the stable, keeping company to three cows and two horses. A miserable night it was too, what with unpleasant odors, constant stamping of hoofs and little flees and bugs crawling all over us. But this was better than staying outside and freezing, at least so we figured.

The third day of our journey passed on without any special discomfort. When we reached a small Arabian town the chief here also offered Miss Mather his home. You see, being an American missionary and dressed as such, she was easily recognized and respected by the majority of the Mohammedans and Arabs. This chief was a kind man and consented to Miss Mather's wishes of having us girls with her.

He took us to his home, just a small room with no windows or any outside opening, except the very small and low doorway through which we had entered. A burning kerosene lamp showed us five women seated on the floor, each garbed in simple Afghans and each wearing a heavy veil, which they removed upon seeing that there were no men folk among us. It proved that these women were the chief's wives. Further we noticed that the floor was earthen and completely bare. We could already feel the chilling dampness. Wearily we spread out our blankets and sat down.

Our host, the chief, was seated on the floor a few feet away holding his hands over a small hole about a foot deep in the floor, which contained some charcoal fire. Presently his wives stepped into a somewhat mysterious looking hole in the wall, which I had presumed was a cupboard, and disappeared. For a while we heard them moving overhead, then suddenly everything was dead silence.

We felt tired and drowsy and made signs of retiring for the night. Still our host sat there staring at us, his inseparable sword beside him. Even with Miss Mather right there with us we were actually afraid of this man and didn't dare go to sleep. After all, he was an Arab and Arabs are just as unwelcome to us as the Turks. What if he should take a fancy to get up in the middle of the night and behead us all in our sleep? These things were being done. I shuddered and wished I were outside or some other place. But I was tired, so very tired, and lay down determined not to go to sleep. Soon the silence and the steady breathing of my three companions told me that they were in deep slumber. I lay there listening to their rhythmic breathing and trying to keep an eye on the Arab seated only a few feet away, a sneering smile on his lips. But I must have fallen asleep, because when I next opened my eyes, a bit surprised, I saw the door was wide open and it was daylight outside, and the chief wasn't in the room. We never did know just when he did leave us.

During the next two days of our journey things went on pretty fairly, considering the many hardships and inconveniences which we had to endure, due to increasing rough roads, and to the fact that we were in constant fear of encountering some malicious highway bandits. And, we would have too, the very next day, if it hadn't been for the timely warning of a fellow traveler coming from the opposite direction just before we started out early the next morning.

In order to escape the outlaws, and possible massacre, we chose a road, which probably had not seen more than a score of travelers in the course of its history. In brief, our choice was a series of hills, which we had to ascend or descend. Then, to make matters worse, we were confronted with a mountain. Wearily we began to ascend single file, on mules, on the foot wide road belting it.

I believe that the crossing of this mountain was really the highlight of our six days of journey from Turkey to Syria. The perilous and uncertain road on which we were gambling our lives is still a nightmare to me. I shiver at the very thought. There we were, lined up on the narrow path, literally suspended in mid air. On our right side, the majestic mountain was towering high above and looked as though it were going to collapse on us, while on our left there was nothing. Nothing, but the bottomless, black pit below, yawning so hungrily at us. I thought of the first day of our journey when my mule had so suddenly decided to repose in the middle of the road. What if he should get such a notion now? I shuddered and held on to the saddle so tight all through the ordeal that I was rewarded with two hands full of aching blisters.

At 1:30 a.m., seven hours late according to schedule, we reached the inn. None of us could sleep a wink that night, we were too upset, although we had outwitted the bandits.

The afternoon of the following day found us in Aleppo, Syria. Miss Mather immediately put me and the other girl from the orphanage on the first train going to Beirut, where we were to get a new passport to America, as our affidavit from Turkey had already expired.

My companion and I were utterly bewildered at the very sight of the train. Why we hadn't even heard of such a thing that could run by itself without the aid of any mules. This must be a miracle. Filled with thrills and amazement, we reached Beirut in nineteen hours. A young man from the Near East Relief was at the station to meet us. Thoughtful Miss Mather had wired them of our coming. As we were attired in the customary orphan's uniforms, he readily recognized us.

The Near East Relief lost no time in proceeding with the business of obtaining our necessary traveling papers. When we applied to the proper authorities for them, we were rudely told that being considered foreigners it was absolutely necessary for us to reside in Syria for at least six months before we could even file for passports. This came to us as a blow. Where were we to stay all that time? Discouraged and sick at heart, we returned to the Relief Office. There was nothing we could do but wait.

The good missionaries placed me and my friend in an American 'Nursery' sort of an orphanage which in reality was just a stop over residence for any travelers connected in any way with the Near East Relief or the Red Cross.

It was a lonely life that we led here as everything was so strange. Even the meals served by an Assyrian cook, were so different from the meals we knew that we simply could not eat them. We lived mostly on fruits and vegetables to which we were accustomed in Turkey.

Then there was the problem of language. We could not speak a word of Arabic, the language used in Beirut, and there wasn't an Assyrian who could speak our tongue. All our thoughts and wishes were expressed in pantomime, the best we could.

Naomi's Story

The six long months having wearily passed, a representative from the Near East Relief once more presented us to the proper officials, reminding them of our intention of applying for passports. This time we were told that as their quota of granting passports had already been exhausted, we must go back to Aleppo to obtain ours. We implored in vain—their word was final. We had to return to Aleppo.

The authorities here also refused to grant us our passports and advised us to return to Beirut. Really this was getting to be a joke, as the Americans expressed it. It made them rather angry. They took the matter in hand and virtually demanded that the authorities favor us with our traveling document. First they emphatically opposed but finally agreed. It was exactly one whole month before the transaction was completed as the officials took their time in signing our papers, sometimes telling us to come back the next day. We returned to Beirut and waited the arrival of the boat that would carry us across the Mediterranean Sea.

At last the happy day came. Just before boarding the boat we were obliged to undergo the usual physical and educational examinations. Everything went on smoothly, until the specialist examined our eyes. Here was a great disappointment in store for us. The doctor announced that our eyes had 'trachoma', a very contagious eye disease and therefore we must remain in Beirut and have them treated.

This required five weeks at the rate of four painful treatments daily. How much I had suffered during these weeks of treatment can never be told in mere words. Indeed I had given up all hopes of ever seeing again. I was certain I would become blind. I was also losing all hopes of ever reaching America, where my beloved Miss Mather had already gone months ago. But, the Lord had intended differently for me. At the end of six weeks, the doctors once more examined my eyes and announced their complete cure. My girl companion was also cured. We were now permitted to sail, however, while our eyes were being treated we missed the boat and had to wait for the next boat.

The day of sailing was, I think, the happiest and the most thrilling day I had ever experienced. The boat was to leave at 4:00 PM. About noon, a representative from the Near East Relief called for us and took us on a shopping tour. He bought each of us a suitcase, coat, hat, a pair of shoes and several changes of clothes. I couldn't believe my sudden riches. I had never before seen so many new clothes all at one time. I was utterly filled with excitement. We spent the remaining hour just looking at hundreds of beautiful things and enjoyed ourselves.

At last we were heading for the docks. With every step I became more and more thrilled, my heart beating so fast and hard as though it were going to burst with sheer joy. What was it like to ride on a boat with nothing but miles and miles of water all around? We were almost there. We could even see the many giant boats lined up along the piers. One of them would soon be carrying us across the sea. My heart throbbed with excitement.

Just as we were hurrying down the busy street leading to the docks our escort met a dear friend of his whom he hadn't seen for several years. As luck would have it, in his sudden joy, he forget his mission and standing in the middle of the road, talked with his friend a long time. My girl companion and I became very anxious as the precious minutes ticked swiftly by. The huge dock clock was about to chime the hour of four. Still our entrusted escort talked. Apparently he had forgotten that we were to sail at 4:00 o'clock.

The shrill whistle of the boat about to depart awakened him to his senses. Grabbing our suitcases and leaving his bewildered friend standing there on the spot, he ran for the boat, while we frantically tried to follow his flying steps. We reached the boat just as they were pulling the gangplank away. After shouting a few excited words in Arabic to the attendants, he took us to the deck and handing us our suitcases and our passports, rushed away and disappeared in the crowd below. The boat began to move and an hour or so later we lost complete sight of land.

We two orphans just stood there on the deck wondering what we should do next. No doubt there was a cabin reserved for us but how were we to find it? We had never set foot on a boat before, we didn't even know what cabins were. Who could we go to for help?—There wasn't a person on the boat who spoke our language. We stood there, helpless, away from the crowd.

Presently a man in uniform came toward us and motioning to our suitcases began talking rapidly. We didn't have the slightest idea what he was saying, but handed him our passports hoping me might help us find our cabin. He looked at us a bit surprised then beckoned us to follow him.

We went down a long and narrow hallway and stopped in front of a door numbered 29. He motioned us to go in and went on his way. When we tried to open it we found that it was locked. Timidly we knocked and the door flew open, disclosing a very excited and angry man raving away in a language unknown to us. Picking up our suitcases, we walked into the room, but like a mad man, he chased us out. Surprised, we tried to tell him that this was our cabin, showing him the number on the door and the corresponding number on our passports. This seemed to make no difference to him. Still shouting with anger, he went in slamming the door after him. My companion and I went back to the deck brooding over our tough luck.

Nightfall came and the evening grew chilly. Presently the whole deck was deserted. Oh well, we couldn't sit here all night. We must find a warm place to sleep. We went down to the dining room carrying our suitcases along. We each had a blanket given to us at the orphanage. Spreading one on the floor and covering ourselves with the other, we waited for blessed sleep to come and give temporary relief to our misfortune.

During the day we would aimlessly roam the decks, each holding on to her suitcase containing her worldly possessions. We must have represented a picture of comedy forever parading up and down the long deck, for our fellow passengers would point at us and laugh. At night we would return to the dining room and retire to 'bed'. We followed this simple routine for seven days and nights crossing the Mediterranean Sea.

About noon on the eighth day we lowered anchor at Marseille, France. How good it was to see land again. My friend and I left the ship following the example of many passengers. There were about twenty horse drawn carriages on the dock, all hopefully prospecting business.

Here the people were speaking French, which was all Chinese to us as far as understanding it was concerned. Uncertain as to what we should do, we walked around looking very much like two lost children, when we heard someone speaking Armenian. Soon a carriage stopped by us and two Armenian men offered us their services. This was the fist time in eight months that we met someone who could speak our language—we almost cried with joy.

Showing our passports we told them that we were going to America and how helpless we were as we didn't know anything about boat schedules. Kindly they told us not to worry, assuring us that they would take care of everything. They drove us to a lodging house and informed us that in a week we'd be sailing over the Atlantic Ocean. Although we were in Marseille a whole week and the people, the beautiful buildings, and many interesting things simply fascinated us, we did not dare venture away from the house for fear we might get lost.

Finally the day of sailing arrived. We were about to take the last step which would bring us to America. Our two Armenian friends drove us to the boat.

Here also the passengers were required to undergo the necessary examinations before boarding the boat. My heart sank. What if the doctor should find something wrong with my eyes? Meekly my girl companion and I went in waiting our fate. After careful examination, the doctor announced that my friend still had signs of 'trachoma' and must remain in Marseille. My eyes however passed the test. Vaccinating me on the right arm for goodness knows what, they put me on the boat. A few hours later I was waving a sad farewell to my unfortunate and tearful friend standing on the dock. That was the last I saw or even heard of her.

I was now completely alone with a long journey ahead, and not a soul speaking my language. Even the three women who occupied the same cabin I did, spoke a different language.

I never knew it was ever possible that anyone could be so utterly miserable and lonely as I, on that first day and all through the seventeen long days and nights that followed. All day long I would stand on the deck leaning against the railing and gaze at the heaving green water hundreds of miles around. Timid and shy as I was, I would have strived to make the acquaintance of any stranger for mere company's sake, had I found one who could speak my language. But alas, there were none. Indeed, I felt so miserable that many times I wished I had never left the orphanage and started on such a wretched journey. Would this ocean trip ever end? Would we ever see land again? For fourteen long days we had seen nothing but water, water, water. How many more days were ahead I was unable to find out. Nerve wrecked and driven to tears of distraction, I retired to my cabin.

About seven o'clock the next morning, I was suddenly awakened by a splash of cold water on my face. No sooner had I opened my eyes and, dazed, tried to collect my senses, when another stream

Naomi's Story

of water poured itself into the cabin through the porthole. Now fully awake I could hear excited voices and hurried steps running back and forth out in the hall. My roommates were also awake now. Murmuring, they hurriedly dressed and rushed out. Puzzled and curious, I followed them. As I stepped through the door something seemed to jerk me and I staggered and nearly fell against the side of the hall. Strange, I felt all right, yet I couldn't stand on my feet. I seemed to rock so.

Somehow I reached the deck where all the commotion was. There I witnessed some two hundred hysterical passengers, screaming and running back and forth, while the cool headed deck stewards vainly attempted to calm them down. In a moment I realized that we were helplessly marooned in a hectic ocean storm.

The mighty Atlantic had wrathfully transformed itself into roaring little mountains of water and tons upon tons of thunderous water mercilessly beat against the massive ship with terrific force, threatening to pull her and her handful of pitiful humanity down, down into the black unfathomable depths of a watery grave. How the angry ocean heaved. First it seemed to swell up on one side away from us then roll down straight at us with thunderous roar, almost capsizing the huge liner. Already a violent wind had risen, lending a destructive hand for our doom. The immense ship was like a piece of wood, helplessly caught in a whirlpool.

Next it started to rain. The frenzied people, like rats caught in a trap, were crying and praying at the same time. Several persons, crazed with fear, ran over to the railings and tried to jump overboard. I stood silently by, my eyes fixed on the foaming green waters.

The boat wasn't progressing at all now but only rocking from side to side by the force of the raged waves. The Captain came down and excitedly talked to the deck hands, who immediately brought forth the life preservers and handed one to each passenger. Few of the crew were busy lowering the life boats.

I wonder if the reader can possibly feel, or even imagine, the gravity of such a moment, as we realized with a sickening sensation, that we had only a few minutes of life left to us, and that in less than an hour our warm living bodies would be hurled into the icy waters of a roaring ocean, there to remain forever and slowly rot. As I stood there expecting the worst, I lost all hopes of seeing America or the aunt who had sent for me. In my mind I lived again my twelve years of life. True, the Lord had saved me from exile—I had escaped the massacre of 1920—I was unharmed when the forty Turkish bandits attacked us on the first day of our journey—I had survived the perilous trip over the mountains and had safely crossed the Mediterranean Sea. But this—who could escape the fury of a mighty ocean? Surely this was the end of my journey and of my life. In a few hours perhaps, I would be no more.

But fate had intended differently. Gradually the threatening winds died down and the furious destructive mountains of water slowly settled to their natural level. Coaxingly the ship pushed herself forward, and in a few hours we were once more smoothly sailing ahead with a prayer of thanks on each passenger's lips.

On the morning of October 31, 1922, three days after the storm, we sighted a few birds flying in the sky and my sense of reasoning told me that we were near land. Sure enough late that afternoon we could see the thin border of land against the far horizon. Immediately a feeling of security came over me. How good it would feel to stand on safe dry land again.

America! I was about to enter the magic country of the world. As we neared the great harbor of Providence, Rhode Island, the many towering skyscrapers looming so majestically up into the sky simply took my breath away. I had never even imagined that people could build such tall buildings. Knowing nothing of elevator service at the time, I pitied the people who had to climb the hundreds of steps to reach the top floors. Was surprisingly ignorant of the thousand and one other such miracles that were awaiting me in this land of wonders. I could hardly wait to get off the boat.

But suddenly a pang of distress shot through me heart. Where would I go after leaving the boat? As far as I knew nobody would be on the deck to meet me. I started to cry. But I might have spared all my tears and worries because no sooner had the great ship pulled to the dock when officers, after inspecting each passenger's passport, directed us into different departments.

I was duly transferred by truck along with fifteen others, to Boston, Mass., to what proved to be an immigration station. After putting me through a general quiz, they took me to a huge room where, it seemed to me, refugees from all nations had gathered. Several hundred people were at this place, yet not one among them spoke my language. Of the meals served to us by our keepers, there were very few things I could eat, as most of the cooked meals were new and disagreeable to me. In the way of beds, the only thing furnished to us were the bedsprings, in bunk form. Everyone had to supply his own bedding or go without. Wrapping my blanket around me each night vainly I'd try to sleep in one of these bunks. Generally speaking I spent a very unfavorable time here.

Thirteen such miserable days I lived through. Then on November 13, after questioning me as to where and to whom I was going, (all through an interpreter) the officials in charge put me on a train headed for Chicago, Illinois.

The ensuing trip proved to be very tedious and lonely. As the train slowed down at its destination I commenced to cry, being at a complete loss as to what I should do upon leaving the train. The kind conductor wrote my name on a slip of paper and pinned it on my shoulder. Wearily I stepped down onto the platform.

As I walked down the length of the depot, amazed at the wonders all around me, I forgot my troubles temporarily. Heedlessly I walked, marveling at this, that, and everything. Presently a young man advancing in my direction looked at the written name on my shoulder and motioned me to follow him. I obliged him, although I had no idea who he was. Two blocks away we stopped a lady who apparently had been waiting for us. After exchanging a few words to her, the young man left, leaving me with this stranger. I didn't know what it was all about. I could neither speak nor understand English. The best I could do was to recite the alphabet.

Taking me by the hand my lady escort led me to her office. Here much to my relief, was an interpreter who threw some light on the mystery. It proved that this office was a Near East Relief branch to who my aunt from Seattle had wired, informing them of my coming and requesting them to kindly look after me, and see that I got on the right train. Accordingly, about 11:00 PM, these good people put me on the train, showed me the berth reserved for me and told me that in six days I would see my aunt. At last I was on the final step of my long journey.

However, this very last stretch of my travel on the train did not meet any enthusiasm on my part. I was so lonely and wished for the day when I'd set foot in Seattle, thus ending my misery, the misery that I have been enduring since the day I left Turkey ten months ago. Having nothing to do, or to read or anyone to speak to, I'd sit by the window from morning till night, just gazing away.

The porter, who had been told by the missionaries at the station to look after me, would good-naturedly bring my meals on a tray and coax me to eat.

One day, two American ladies, noticing me sitting at the window day after day, came over and cheerfully began talking, but I only stared at them, not having the faintest idea of what they were saying. Then they kindly offered me an open box of chocolate drops. I had never seen or tasted chocolates in my life, so naturally, not knowing what they were at the time, I refused. Much amused at my continued silence and hopeless timidity, they walked away and deposited the box of candy into the hands of the surprised, but pleased, porter standing nearby.

The sixth day, November 18, 1922, happily marked the end of my journey, thus leaving the cruel old country behind me forever, and starting a new and happier life in a new wonderful country—America. As the train slowed down, the jolly porter told me to get ready, that we were now in Seattle, Washington. A feeling of unspeakable thrill came over me. I had on the same dress and coat that I did in Chicago, as the kind missionaries had bid me to do, because they had wired a brief description of me and of my clothes to my aunt as her only means of recognizing me.

As soon as I appeared in the doorway leading down to the platform, I heard a feminine voice cry out in Armenian "There she is— there she is." The next moment a strong hand grasped me by the wrist, pulling me down. Before I realized it, I was in the arms of my tearful, but happy, aunt, so closely resembling my beloved mother. Speechless by the ecstasy of our reunion, we entered into the waiting car of a friend and hurriedly drove home, where a feast of Armenian foods awaited me.

The next day was devoted to many curious neighbors and friends who came to see me. I felt like an object on exhibition. And, my appearance must have justified my feelings, as I stood there, rather small in stature but generously plump, dressed in a pink sateen dress, white shoes and white stockings, and two black husky braids hanging nonchalantly over my shoulders, because visitors looked at me and chuckled, highly amused. I was deluged with questions regarding my country and my journey to America and everything I said had to be translated to English by my aunt.

Two weeks later my auntie took me to a beauty shop and relieved me of my long hair. The next few days were spent wholly in having a good time and getting accustomed to the new life before me. Truly, this was the land of miracles. Everywhere I looked I saw the work of wonders (bright electric lights, the magic moving pictures, telephones, into which I was afraid to talk for a long time, the street cars, the radios, the gas stoves, the automobiles, and those wonderful canned goods, and countless other things)—all of them such welcome agents in saving time and trouble to the civilized and carefree American people. All these things simply took my breath way, to say nothing of the shops full of ready-made clothes, hats, toys and thousands of other articles so temptingly on display for sale. But, what completely bewildered me were the huge life size models in the shop windows displaying dresses, coats, etc. Unaware of the important purpose they were executing and presuming that they were there for sale, I wondered what manner of person could and would play with such big dolls.

Another thing that utterly puzzled me was that everybody wore shoes and stockings all day long, whether they were going away or staying at home. In my country everyone went barefoot. The only time we wore stockings (knitted at home) and shoes, was when we went visiting and during severe cold in the winter. Although, since my arrival to America, I had been dutifully wearing these 'essential' footers. One day, I took them off and went about the streets without them, much to my aunt's horrors. I just couldn't get used to the idea. Patiently auntie explained to me that this was one of the many, many, things that I'd have to get used to doing in America.

It is important for me to describe how different this life was from the life I had known in Turkey. Perhaps my reader can best visualize the vast change if he imagined himself to be suddenly transferred from his utmost modern life to that of a humble and rather primitive life, and try to adjust himself to it accordingly. Such was the situation that confronted me, only in my case it was visa-versa.

After the Christmas holidays, I entered school. Here the teachers faced a serious consideration. Although I had attended seven years of schooling in Turkey, now I had to start over almost from the very beginning due to my inability to speak the English language. Not knowing just what grade I belonged to, they started me off in 4-B. Indeed I felt out of place, a girl of thirteen years, among a score of small children who knew more about their school work than I ever hoped to learn.

I was the victim of much ridicule and jest, as I vainly attempted to use the proper words in answering the occasional questions asked by the teacher. This did not discourage me—instead, it made me realize all the more how important, how absolutely essential, it was to use correct grammar. I resolved to go through school and learn to speak correct English, no matter how hard I would find this to be. My teachers were very patient with me and repeatedly told me I was progressing splendidly. I studied faithfully and painstakingly, and during the following year and a half, I satisfactorily completed the fourth, fifth, sixth and the seventh grades. This might seem a bit unreasonable to my readers, but please bear in mind that I had gone through those grades in my country, and now the difference of language was my only handicap.

The first few months of early 1923 were quite blissful and happy ones, in spite of my trying to learn the English language, and the immense task of adjusting myself to the new life before me. There was so much to see and to learn. I was constantly comparing this new and wonderful life—the clothes we wore, the variety of the foods, the stores, the schools, everything—to the simple and semi-civilized life I knew in Turkey, and it was all so frightening, like a huge mountain before me that I must climb. It was a heavy burden on my shoulders.

In addition to this frustration, there was yet more trouble to come. Lately I noticed a great change in my aunt's attitude toward me. Instead of being pleased at my excellent school work, she seemed very irritated. Everything I said or did seemed to aggravate her. I could see no cause for this change in her toward me. I felt I was a big help to her in keeping up the house. She began to ignore me more and more every day. She made me feel I was an outsider. There were no more trips to town with her. She would go and leave me alone. I could not help feeling the terrible, uneasy tension between us. Conditions and the unbearable tension between us became more and more intolerable, and finally wound up to a shocking climax.

PART II

Oh, those Stormy Mistreatment Years, 1923–1924

As time went on, I suffered many mistreatments at the hand of my aunt. I will mention a few here that are still so vivid in my mind, and that I will never forget.

One Saturday morning uncle Mesrop (my aunt's first husband) before leaving the house, had left 30 cents on the table for me to go to the Queen Anne Theatre to see the show that afternoon. I told auntie I didn't know how to get to the theatre. She said, "That's too bad—you can stay home and clean the house." She picked up the money and went downtown alone and was gone all day.

Then there was the incident about the bright red velvet hat she had bought for me. I hated it. She knew how I hated to wear a hat—or even a scarf over my head. One bright sunny spring day I went to school—only one and a half blocks away—without my hat. When I came home for lunch, she was waiting for me in the kitchen, with my hat in her hand, and said very angrily, "So you went to school without your hat," and gave me a hard slap on my left cheek.

Then, the thing that hurt me the most was about my suitcase with which I had traveled halfway around the world, from the orphanage in Marash, Turkey to America, and which contained all my dearest possessions—souvenirs, pictures, Armenian laces, things that were given to me by my friends in the orphanage, the gingham uniform that I wore while there, and the beautiful red wool sweater from Germany, given to me with such high honors—all were in that suitcase which I had put out of the way in the attic. One day as I came home from an errand, I saw that she had thrown the whole thing—suitcase and all—in the garbage can. I dared not to take it out for fear she would slap my face again. It was her way of hurting me. I went to my room and cried my heart out.

I am now in the 7th grade and am about 14 years old—much older than my classmates because of my language handicap. In our sewing class the teacher said we were going to make bloomers (style of the era then) and for everyone to bring black Sateen. I came home and told my aunt about it. The next day she went downtown and came home with small package, and throwing it at my face said, "Here, make your bloomers with this." I looked inside and saw that she had bought white Indian Head Material. At class the next day I pulled out the white material out of the bag and the whole class roared with laughter. I was so humiliated, and the tears swelled in my eyes. The teacher quieted the class but didn't say anything to me. She knew of my problems at home.

The situation between Auntie and me was getting to the breaking point. My very presence seemed to antagonize her. At dinner time she would scold me and make some cruel remarks about me, forcing the tears in my eyes and a lump in my throat while I tried to swallow the food. Uncle Mesrop, of course, would never interfere at any time. She made me feel as if I was a piece of rotten meat under her nose, and wanted to get rid of me. The situation between us got so bad, that at one time I even considered committing suicide by poison.

Things finally came to a head early in January 1924. I came home from school one day and told Auntie that my teacher wanted me to open a school bank account so that I could deposit 10 or 15 cents every Tuesday like the rest of the children so that the class could have 100% banking. She looked at me with fiery eyes and said, "I spent $500.00 to bring you here from Turkey, now you want a bank account. Well, you can have your bank account, but you are going out and work for your room and board—there will be no more school for you." A few months later when school was out in June, I was watering the front yard when a gray-haired, kind looking elderly lady came up the street and went into our home. I though she was just another customer coming to look at some Oriental rugs, and maybe buy one (my aunt and uncle were in that business). Soon Auntie came to the front door and called me in. We went to the living room and my aunt said, "This is the girl." Mrs. Bowden (that was the lady's name) looked at me and said, "Why she is only a child, what can she do?." Auntie said, "Don't let her size fool you, she is a good worker." I didn't know what this was all about. Mrs. Bowden held a copy of the weekly Queen Anne District Newsletter in which my aunt had put an ad—SCHOOL GIRL WANTS STEADY HOUSE WORK. Of course, I didn't know anything about this. Mrs. Bowden looked at the ad in her hand, then looked at me and said, "No, I don't think she will do—I have a big two-story house and my rule is that my kitchen and bathroom have to be scrubbed every Wednesday and Saturday." I said to Mrs. Bowden in my broken English and very heavy accent, "Here I scrub the floors whenever they need it." She looked at me in amazement, and shaking her right forefinger at me said, "You'll do—you come work for me." And so, I left my aunt's home and went with Mrs. Bowden to work for her and her husband in the big two-story home in the Capital Hill District, far away from Queen Anne Hill District where my aunt lived.

During the long weeks that followed, I literally lived in a daze. I just could not believe the turn of the affairs had taken. I didn't even know the damaging cause of it all. The heartache and the wretched loneliness that I experienced on the day I lost my family forever, came over me again. Here I was, in a new country, friendless, so totally unfamiliar with its laws and rules, facing a life so completely different from the humble life I knew, and getting such a pitiful start working as a maid, among strangers. It wasn't so much the principle of my working that hurt me, but the circumstances, the cruel, mocking circumstances of which I became the victim, that was breaking my heart with sorrow. Perhaps fate was playing a practical joke on me. Odd, how I was spared the horrors and tortures of exile and after living for five and a half years in the orphanage, made that unforgettable journey halfway around the world and came to my aunt with hopes for a happier life, only to face such a tragic disappointment, to have these happy dreams and hopes shattered into a million bits. Surely fate was ridiculing my life.

Even greater than this disappointment was the one thing that repeatedly burned through my mind—'no more school for you—no more school for you'. Knowing that in the old country it was up to the parents whether or not their children should have an education, I presumed it was the same in this country. It was absurd! True, during the year and a half in this country I had learned enough English to get by, but I could not yet speak intelligently. If I were to make my way in this new land, surely I had many things to learn yet. Fortunately the family I was working for treated me kindly and said that I could stay with them and work my way through school if I wished.

As the hot summer months rolled by and September came, I entered the eighth grade. To work thus, and to keep up my school work, especially when I had to study so hard in order to keep up with the rest of the class, was sometimes almost more than I could bear. I spent many a tearful night over my books but I was determined to finish grade school, at least.

Early the following October (1924), my uncle died, and auntie sent for me. She said I could now come back and stay with her on the condition that I give up the idea of continuing my schooling. I could not for the life of me understand why she insisted on taking me out of school. To this day I am of the opinion that she gave me this option as a means of temptation, because she knew I was painfully shy and bitterly disliked being among strangers.

I stood there considering. Yes, it was hard to work and live with strangers, and I much preferred to stay with my aunt. But what would my life be in the future without a bit of education? I could not just indefinitely depend on her or anyone else for my support. There would come a time when I'd have to make my way in this world. I could see nothing for the future as long as I lived with my aunt and completely gave up my schooling. We'd even speak our native language daily, thus hindering my English which was so essential to me in the new country.

My mind was made up. I stood up and facing my aunt bravely said, "Auntie, I am willing to continue to work for my room and board and go through school." She looked surprised, as if she hadn't heard me correctly. Then she walked over to me and delivering a stunning blow on the back of my neck said, "Alright go and get your education, but don't you ever dare come back to my house," and with that she put me out of her home.

Sullenly I returned to the family where I worked and going up to my room, cried my heart out. It was hard to believe that my aunt, the one and only relative left to me in this world and who had so graciously brought me from the other end of the globe, could treat me so. Ah, dear reader, it is torture for me to live all this over as I write it down, but that's what my whole life has been, a series of mental tortures. So far life had offered me neither happiness nor peace of mind. With the growing years I seem to realize more and more the importance of family life. I had a family once, a family of seven fond members, each so endearing to my heart, of which I was so cruelly robbed and which since 1917 has been only a sweet memory to me.

In June 1925, I graduated from grade school. Not quite satisfied, I wished to acquire two years of high school education. In order to carry out my ambitions, it was necessary for me to change residence. By the aid of the newspaper advertisements. I moved into a new family and the following September entered high school.

I selected to follow the Commercial Course. Although my studies now were even harder and some of my subjects very trying at times, I was still determined to continue for at least two years, and I did. I could never have accomplished this if it had not been for the kind and unceasing help bestowed upon me by Mr. and Mrs. K. Dehn, the couple for whom I was working. From the very start Mrs. Dehn seemed to be very interested in my welfare and in my schooling, and repeatedly reminded me to feel free to go to her for any help I may need. Many an evening Mr. Dehn spent long hours working out some puzzling problems, writing business letters or helping me with the bookkeeping. It was due to their exhaustive and friendly help that I went through these two years without a single failure in any of my subjects.

By this time I believed I was sufficiently prepared to acquire a position and thus take my first step in self supporting. But, Mrs. Dehn thought to the contrary. She talked some sense into my head and encouraged my further education. She said I had reached the half way mark, the hardest part, and that it would be very foolish for me to quit now. She showed me the dire necessity in my case, of acquiring a complete high school education.

Of course, I would finish my school. How could I do otherwise when dear Mrs. Dehn pleaded with me so? During my two years stay with her I had developed such a keen love and gratitude for all that she had done for me, and had become so fond of her, that any wish of hers regardless of its nature, I gladly obliged. I would give my life's blood for her, were it deemed necessary to do so. Life is a queer thing. Here was a stranger for whom I worked as an insignificant orphan, who patiently pleaded with me urging me to finish my schooling, yet it was for this very same principle that my aunt who had brought me from the other end of the world, put me out of her home.

In 1929 I graduated from Queen Anne High School in Seattle, Washington. I am vain enough to admit that I was quite proud of my achievement. I sent my aunt an invitation to the commencement exercises, to which she readily responded. She congratulated me and invited me to visit her whenever I wished.

For the next six years I had taken advantage of this invitation and visited my aunt quite frequently. On various occasions she gave me the impression that she would prefer to have me go back to her, mildly hinting that I shouldn't be among strangers. But, how could I? She seemed to have forgotten the little misunderstanding we had a few years earlier. Dear reader, I don't want to seem ungrateful, but many a time my aunt has caused me to regret bitterly that I ever came to this country. I could never, never, live again in the home from which I was once put out, with a painful blow administered on the back of my neck, which still seems to sting at the mere thought of it.

Furthermore, I now had a good position in a reliable company and earned a fair living. The 'strangers' with whom I came in contact in the course of the years, have been very kind to me and I constantly gained new friends. At this time I lived in solitude, making the best of life in general, forever seeking that peace of mind which I felt would never come to me in this world.

I have thus attempted to briefly account for those long torturous years since 1917 when I so tragically lost my entire family in one day. I have not once heard from them or even about them. I do not know whether any of them is living or not. I have lost all traces of my few relatives who survived the horrible massacre in 1920. I am now alone in the world, with a bitter and lonely heart, thanks to the ruthless Mohammedans.

My friends have repeatedly heard my tragic yet adventurous story, as on many occasions I have been privileged to talk about my life to various clubs and church groups. Yes, they have all en-

Naomi's Story

joyed my story and have congratulated me. They have even enthusiastically suggested that I write a book about it. Little do they realize that each time I re-live the past, the deep wound in my heart grows still deeper. I sincerely hope that this is the last time I will go through it all.

Fourteen years have gone by since my arrival in America, and it is now 1936.

I must not fail to mention the high honor bestowed upon me just recently. I know my readers will be interested.

Having successfully passed all the required Federal examinations for citizenship, I have just received my final papers making me a full-fledged American citizen, the most gratifying and dear gift that can be granted to an alien.

America has given me a fair education; a chance to live a normal life and full citizenship. I am proud of my new country. I'm proud to belong to such a wonderful country, a country which has acquired the supremacy of civilization and which is the finest and the greatest country on the face of the earth. I KNOW.

PART III

He Dried My Tears
Dedication to Bernie

This part of my story is dedicated expressly to my wonderful husband, Bernard S. Cohen, affectionately known to every one as just plain "Bernie." He was destined to change the entire course of my life. He had such a sunny, pleasant personality, always so full of fun and laughter. Wherever he showed up, a happy smile would instantly light up over everyone's face, and he would be affectionately greeted with "Hi Bernie."

Needless to say that my personality was quite the opposite—me being the sad, quiet, shy, melancholy and reserved type. His coming into my life in 1942 was good for me. Even though deep down inside of me was the heart-breaking past, the tragedy of the unknown whereabouts of my entire family (always wondering what happened to them all) forever gnawing at my heart, Bernie taught me how to laugh again.

Bernie coming into my life was as if he had found me in a dark, cold, fathomless cave, and had brought me into the warm, bright sunshine, with his complete devotion and endearing love. But, read on dear friend.

How swiftly has time rolled into oblivion. Nineteen years have already melted away into the past since my arrival in America, now it is the year 1941—a year to be long remembered for generations to come, the world over. The daily newspapers and radios were full of news of the cruel war that has been raging in Europe for the past four or five years. However, the war overseas hadn't affected the lives of the American people much, and everyone went about their work at a normal pace. But, having lived through the

Naomi's Story

World War 1 while living in Turkey, and losing my entire family of seven in 1917, and again living through that horrible massacre in 1920 while living in the Bethel Orphanage, I prayed to God every day and night, and hoped that America did not get involved in this war in progress. This icy fear was always in my heart. Lord, don't let it happen again. I just could not go through another war.

But the long arm of the insidious was already reaching over the American horizon, and then the incredible happened on the morning of Sunday, December 7, 1941—Japan's surprise bombing of Pearl Harbor, Hawaii.

How well I remember that fateful day. It was on a Sunday morning about 9:30 a.m. I had been invited for breakfast at some dear friend's home, and we were all sitting at the table eating while listening to the church service on the radio, when suddenly the program stopped, and a radio bulletin screamed the terrible news of Japan's sneak attack on our Naval Base in Pearl Harbor. It was as if a bomb had suddenly been dropped on our heads. No one could eat another bite of food. In no time at all, newspapers all over the country were printing extras with screaming headlines, and the radios were constantly broadcasting the extensive damage done to our dozens of war-ships, practically all of them completely demolished and sunk, and of the thousands of our service men losing their lives. December 7th will always be remembered as a black day in America, with the slogan "Remember Pearl Harbor" on every American's lips.

The next day, Monday, December 8th, 1941, was to be a very memorable day making U.S. history. I remember that I was at work at the blouse factory, with everyone silently going about their work with a heavy heart. About 10:00 A.M. all the power machines stopped, and a fearful hush fell over the factory. The news over the office radio announced that the president of the United States, Franklin D. Roosevelt, would now speak to the people of our nation. We all knew what was coming, and with a sickening heart, waited for the dreadful words. After a lengthy speech he declared United States at war with Japan, thus taking us into World War II. It rocked the country. We were stunned, but knew in our hearts that a war was inevitable.

The government lost no time in drafting our men and young boys by the hundreds of thousands, to be sent overseas to fight the Japanese. They were called from their businesses, offices and factories. And, of course, men from airplane factories were no exceptions. Productions of war-arms, ships, and planes were stepped up tremendously. As our men were drafted for war, more and more women were being hired by all manufacturers, including airplane factories. Because I knew what war was all about, I decided to work in a plane factory, and in my very small way, help my wonderful adopted country, America.

I started by first telling my boss at the blouse factory that I wished to put in my application for work at Boeing, in the production department. I also told my boss that if I couldn't get on at Boeing, or if I wasn't able to do the work assigned to me, I would like to come back and work for him again. You see, because I am an orphan and completely self-supporting, I believe in always leaving an open door, because jobs for me were very hard to get. The odds were stacked up against me—my heavy accent, my pitiful shyness, and above all, my size. You see, I'm only 4'10" tall. My boss assured me that my job at his factory was always there for me, for as long as I wanted, and complimented me by saying that I was his best hand-finisher, and he hated to lose me.

In March, 1942, three months after the United States declared war on Japan, I applied for work at Boeing. I was turned down. They wouldn't even take my application. But, I would not give up. I kept going back over and over again, telling them that I would even clean the ladies' restroom, if they would only give me a chance. Finally on June 3, 1942, I was hired as a rivet-bucker. I had no idea what a rivet-bucker was supposed to do, but I knew I had a job, and I was in my glory. Now I could work in a "defense plant" and do my little bit for my new adopted country.

Entering Boeing Plant II for the first time, was really an experience never to be forgotten. The feeling that came over me was awesome. It was simply stupendous. The endless rows of planes in various stages of production, the thousands of people crawling like ants inside and outside the planes, simply took my breath away. And, the noise, it was deafening.

I was assigned to a girl riveter who checked out several bucking bars, and, climbing inside the plane, showed me how to buck the rivets, while she drove them with her rivet gun from the outside. I never knew what noise was before. Imagine about 20 rivet guns going at one time and 20 buckers bucking rivets inside—and that is only in one small section of the plane. My assignment was in the tail section. At this time we were building B-17's. After 5,000 B-17's, we started building B-29's, bombers.

Naomi's Story

After about three months of bucking rivets, I was promoted to be a riveter. Now I worked on the outside of the tail section, riveting the skin on. This necessitated my climbing on top of the tail section to complete riveting there.

Time went on and after about six months, one day in December, 1942, I had come down from the plane and was at my work bench when a man—a Boeing electrician—stopped by and rattled off a few words in a language I did not understand. In my surprise I turned to him and grunted, "Huh?" He then spoke a few words in a different language and again I shook my head. Then he asked me if I was French—Italian—Spanish—and even Mexican. I shook my head 'no'. He said, "tell me what nationality you are and I'll talk to you in your language, because I can talk in anything but Greek." I told him I was an Armenian. He said, "Well, that's Greek to me," and nonchalantly walked away. I looked after him and thought, huh, a funny man, a joker, and continued with my work. I never realized at that time, he was to be my future husband.

We were entering the second year of war. Production of planes was stepped up, and we put in a lot of overtime, even Saturdays and Sundays. Since I lived alone, and time was my own, I worked whenever they asked me to. One Sunday while having lunch with a couple of girls from my shop, this man—the joker—somehow found me, and sat beside us. He asked me if I remembered him. I said, "Yes." He then introduced himself as Bernie Cohen (Bernard S. Cohen) and I told him my name. He said he would nickname me 'Pigeon', because I reminded him of a pigeon perched on top of a plane. From then on our meeting was a daily thing, having lunch together every day. I must confess I looked forward to seeing him every day too. He had such a marvelous sense of humor, and his capacity for jokes seemed endless. Everyone's face would light up whenever he was around, because we knew we were in for a good laugh. His name and personality were synonymous with laughter. Our personalities were of opposite nature—his happy, devil-may-care type, mine quiet, serious and shy. But, somehow we seemed so suited to each other. We started dating pretty steady. He made me forget that I was an orphan, that I had such a tragic background—losing my entire family of seven during the First World War back in 1917.

The following Spring, April 1943, Bernie took me by surprise by popping the big question, and presented me with a beautiful diamond ring. I was speechless. These things just simply didn't happen to me. But, it was true, it was happening to me. I had grown very fond of Bernie, but marriage had not entered my mind. I was elated, and accepted his proposal.

All over the country, everyone was buying Savings Bonds, and involving themselves in various projects to raise money for "Uncle Sam." Being the kind of person that he was, my Bernie was constantly thinking of ways of raising money in various shops at the plant, thus doing his bit to help "Uncle Sam." He would ask employees to buy savings stamps, towards buying savings bonds, and he would arrange a special ceremony and have the stamps destroyed by burning them, or mixing them in real salad, thus making them useless. In this way the stamps could not be redeemed and Uncle Sam got the money. The various stunts became quite popular, and the Boeing News photographer would take pictures of us for the Boeing News. Bernie and I became quite popular among the employees and at Boeing in general.

While he was thus busy raising money for the war effort, he climaxed the matters by touching a live nerve, asking me to buy a $1,000.00 war bond with my life's savings—approximately $800.00, all money I had saved in 17 years (I was already buying a bond a month). I looked at him speechless, and put up a feeble argument against it. However, his persuasive manner, and the fact that I loved him, won out. I bought the $1,000.00 war bond ($750.00) thus becoming the very first person at Boeing to have done such a thing. The Boeing Newspaper photographer lost no time in coming right down to my shop and taking my picture while riveting. The picture, along with an article about my background, appeared in the next issue, setting me as an example to other employees. Incidentally, this issue was dated June 3, 1943, exactly one year after I was hired at Boeing.

As the Summer gave way to Fall, Bernie and I started planning our forthcoming marriage in January 1944. He made it very clear from the start that it was going to be a big wedding, with nothing spared. He said it would help, in a small way, to make up for the sad life I've had in the past.

I started shopping for my wedding gown and veil, and eventually settled on white chiffon velvet, to be custom made, with a long train, fitted bodice, long sleeves and sweetheart neckline. My lace trimmed telle veil was a beauty in itself, with even a longer train than on my gown, and a huge heart in the center done up in lace. I chose my two bridesmaids, maid of honor, and matron of honor.

Naomi's Story

Bernie lined up his best man, and two ushers. We had wedding invitations printed and mailed out, not forgetting to post one in Bernie's shop, and also one in my shop. The Boeing News put out a wonderful article about us, and, at our request, an open invitation to any employee who cared, to come to our wedding.

About a week before the wedding, Bernie and I were having lunch downtown, when suddenly, he pulled a small package from his pocket and pushed it toward me, saying it was his wedding gift to me. Surprised, I opened it, and found a pair of beautiful, dazzling, diamond earrings. I was so dumb-founded I could not speak. He had noticed that I had pierced ears, and wanted me to put them on before the wedding to see if my ears would hurt. You see, my ears had been pierced when I was a baby—as are all girl babies in the old country. He helped me put them on, and it did not hurt a bit.

On Sunday, January 16, 1944, at 8:00 p.m., we arrived at Temple De Hirsch, to be married. The place was packed to its capacity. I looked over the crowd proudly, when suddenly a twinge of sadness pierced my heart. Bernie's and my family were not there to share our happiness and witness our wedding. As you know, my family of seven had been exiled from Marash, Turkey, in 1917, and presumed all dead. Both of Bernie's parents had died of pneumonia in 1936, (he was orphaned at that time, as he was an only child) long before he came into my life. So, here we were, two orphans getting married—Bernie of Jewish faith, and I of Christian faith, so totally and deeply in love with each other, about to take our marriage vows in the presence of The Almighty God above.

Slowly I walked down the aisle on the arm of my Uncle Dick (my Aunt's second husband). My wedding dress was beautiful. My bridal bouquet was of white gardenias and white rose buds—my favorite flowers. Yes, my Aunt was there too, after all, she had saved me from those barbaric and uncivilized Turks in Turkey, and had brought me from halfway around the world to this wonderful country, America, for which I have been truly grateful, and always will be. Besides, this was a happy occasion, my big day, and I decided to let bygones be bygones.

Instead of the traditional song "Here Comes The Bride" played on the organ, Bernie had requested that the song, "I'll Be Loving You Always", be played on the violin. It was the song that he had courted me with.

A hush fell over the crowd as our song began to play on the violin. As we neared the end of the aisle, my heart began to pound so hard—as if it would burst open. It was so full of love for the man who was waiting there for me, as our beautiful song continued to play ever so softly. I neared Bernie, all dressed in his tuxedo, and never taking his adoring eyes off me, my eyes filled with happy tears. This was real, not a dream. Here was a man who truly loved me and was willing to share his life with me. For the first time in my life, ever since I lost my family, I felt I was loved and wanted. The music stopped and the wedding ceremony started. Twenty minutes later, we were pronounced husband and wife.

Following our wedding was our big reception, and what a reception it was. As Bernie and I led the crowd into the synagogue's huge reception hall and lined up for the receiving line, the five piece orchestra we had hired was already softly playing our theme song—"I'll Be Loving You Always." The tables were set so beautifully—to the last detail. The gorgeous wedding cake was decorated with white sugar rose buds and silver leaves, and the doll figures of the Bride and Groom perched on top. There were two flat matching cakes at each end of the table. We wanted to be sure that our more than 400 well-wishing guests received a piece of wedding cake. There were also the tall, white light candles, tied with white ribbon bows. The refreshments and coffee were catered by the Manning Company personnel.

Everyone was happy, dancing to the soft music of the orchestra, and in between dances there were stage acts, with Bernie as the Master of Ceremony. Yes, this was a very happy occasion, a day to be cherished and remembered forever. Everyone was dancing, laughing and having a wonderful time. I remember there were two photographers from the Boeing News staff, taking various pictures, and pictures of my bridal party. About two weeks later, the staff members presented Bernie and me with beautiful scrapbook. On the cover were two beautiful hand-drawn red hearts, with "Bernie" printed on one, and "Naomi" printed on the other. Inside they had pasted copies of all the articles and pictures of us that had appeared in the Boeing News for the past year. You see, we were quite popular trying to raise money for "Uncle Sam." Finally they had pasted wedding pictures taken at the reception. It was a very thoughtful and endearing gift, one which we would always cherish.

Naomi's Story

As all good things must come to an end, so did our reception. We sneaked out and went back to the apartment, changed clothes and headed for the boat to Vancouver, Canada, where we spent our honeymoon of one week.

Well, even honeymoons must come to an end—and so did ours. We returned to work and settled down to the serious business of doing our part in winning the war.

Having built 5,000 powerful B-17 bombers for the war effort, Boeing had now switched over to building the even more powerful B-29 bombers, and rolling them off the final assembly line as fast as possible. My new assignment on these B-29 bombers was riveting the gun-turret over the nose of the plane. True, it was hard work—I had to use a bigger and more powerful rivet gun to drive those frozen rivets in, but I didn't mind—I could handle it. I felt I was doing my little bit for my adopted country in winning the war—(I also maintained a near perfect attendance record).

We entered the year 1945—a year that was to be remembered forever the world over. People all over the country, in all the "War Plants", were working feverishly to continuously supply our fighting boys with war-ships, ammunitions, and airplanes, etc. There was endless rationing on food, gasoline, etc.

In early August, 1945, (I think it was the 6th) a frightful and incredible thing happened that rocked and stunned the world. The United States had dropped the world's first atomic bomb on Hiroshima, Japan, killing hundreds of thousands of people instantly, and leaving the city in complete ruin. Needless to say, it put an instant end to war with Japan. The news was broadcast to the Boeing employees over the public address system, and immediately all work came to a dead-stop, then everyone was given the rest of the day off. Soon after, the company began to systematically terminate its employees, and on December 12, 1945, I was duly terminated, thus putting an end to my Boeing career (after almost three and a half years).

My husband, Bernie, being a top-rated maintenance electrician, was kept on the permanent payroll at Boeing. How happy I was. Now I could stay home and start raising a family, and somehow fill that empty spot in my heart—left empty since 1917. However, this was never to be. My husband decided to quit Boeing and open an electrical business of his own. As we had very little cash savings, and a few savings bonds, I thought it was unwise to go into business, and urged, cried and begged him to stay at Boeing where he had a steady job, and let me stay home and raise a family. Bernie wouldn't listen to reason, finally he quit his job and hunted around for a small place to set up business in Ballard. This was the start of all our troubles yet to come.

We opened a small shop. Bernie decided that I should stay in the store to answer the phone, wait on customers, and do the bookkeeping (about which I knew nothing) and knew even less about electrical merchandise. He said he would do the wiring jobs away from the shop. Needless to say I hated this set-up. Very little work was coming in, and the merchandise did not move. The overhead expenses were piling up—rent, taxes, cost of merchandise, etc.. I could see nothing but doom ahead, and suggested that we give up the shop before we lost everything. Then to make matters even worse, the Union stepped in and prevented my husband from doing the wiring jobs. My husband tried to reason with them, saying that he was just starting out in business, and that as soon as things got better he could hire union men. The Union wouldn't listen and told him that if he had so much as a half day's work, he had to use a union man to do it for him. This was before the Taft Hartley Law. I sincerely believe that this hassle with the Union was one of the prime factors that contributed to our downfall. Poor Bernie didn't really have a chance to get started.

By now all our savings were gone, and the savings bonds were going fast, even my $1,000.00 bond, to pay the monthly bills, and the payroll. Again I begged and pleaded with Bernie to give up the shop and go back to work. And again he wouldn't listen and told me not to worry. Finally things got to the breaking point at the shop, and at home. Then, I sued him for divorce. But we couldn't live without each other—I loved him too much—and after three days we made up, and he promised to give up the shop. But, the damage was done. All our savings bonds were gone, and we were left virtually penniless. In just two and a half years we were completely broke—to say nothing of my developing high blood pressure, and a murmur of the heart. Finally we gave up the shop and it was in February, 1948, when we declared bankruptcy.

Then came endless days, weeks and months of looking for work, which was very scarce because all of our service men returning from war were given top priority.

I was fortunate, and managed to get a job at Eclipse Manufacturing Company doing hand-finishing on expensive blouses. I was earning only $1.10 an hour, but was grateful for it. At least we could eat and pay the $42.50 monthly rent on our two-bedroom apartment.

Meanwhile, Bernie was still trying to find work. He decided on civil service work, and filled out numerous applications. He took exams which he passed with flying colors. However, he had to wait for an opening, and was told that he would be notified as soon as there was one.

Eventually he was assigned to a job on a temporary basis. This lasted for several years—always on a temporary basis, always a different place. Bernie was getting very discouraged and to add to our already troubled lives, he had to have a second surgery on his spine. He recovered from this, but a year later he had to have surgery again—this time to have two-thirds of his stomach removed because of ulcers, from which he had been suffering for quite some time. I firmly believe that this condition was brought on mainly by aggravation and worry over lack of work, lack of finances and the loss of his business.

Early in 1953 our luck changed and things looked a bit brighter. I received a little raise in wages at the Eclipse—now making $1.25 an hour. Bernie got a Federal Civil Service job assignment at the Seattle port of Embarkation. He was given the impression that the job would be permanent. We were overjoyed. He loved his job, and everything looked rosy. We felt we could now breathe.

We had been living in our two-room apartment for nine years (since our marriage) but I had lived there for another nine years before I was married, making a total of eighteen years there for me. I was getting pretty tired of it, and we were talking about looking for a home of our own. Now that Bernie had a steady job, perhaps I could quit my job and raise a family, which I wanted with all my heart. Though the years had passed swiftly over me, it was not yet too late to have children. We hunted around for several months, and looked at dozens of homes. Finally we found a cozy little house, five years old, with a fireplace (a must) and on August 13, 1953, we moved into our little love nest. The down payment was comparatively small, the monthly payment at $72.00, with the interest rate at 4½%. We were sure we could swing it. We had practically no furniture, but we didn't really mind (there would be plenty of time for that).

We had been in our home only three months when a blow struck us again. President Eisenhower had just ordered 25,000 Federal employees to be terminated up and down the West Coast for what he called 'Reduction In Force'. Because Bernie had been employed less than a year he was among the first to be laid off. We were stunned. What were we going to do now? What other heartaches were in store for us? I still had my $1.25 an hour job at the blouse factory, but that was hardly enough to make the house payments and eat too.

Then, as if by a miracle, two of our very dear friends came to our rescue and each offered to loan us $300.00—without interest—so we could keep up with the mortgage payments for the time being. They said they were in no hurry to get paid back. I was so relieved I cried.

Bernie continued to look for work, but there was none to be had. Discouraged, he decided to drum up his own work, repairing small appliances, lamps, switches and outlets in homes. He managed to keep busy, operating right from his car.

A year or so later, another blow. Bernie was hospitalized again and scheduled for another surgery. I was so worried and torn between staying at my job at the blouse factory, and nursing Bernie back to health upon leaving the hospital. Each surgery left its toll on poor Bernie, and he was gradually slowing down—but not in spirit (that wonderful sense of humor of his). He always had a story to tell to anyone who would listen—even when recuperating, he always had a joke, and I loved him for it. I think that his great sense of humor helped me in carrying my own burden. He was good for me.

We had been in our home about two years. Although Bernie managed to keep busy whenever he was able to work (on his own), money was not easy to come by, and the customers were slow in paying us. I remember the time when our checking account was down to $4.31, and the house payment due, along with all the other bills that came on the first of the month. I also remember phoning the mortgage company on three different occasions, telling them that we could not make our payment on time, and for them to do what they had to do. They were wonderful about it, and told me not to worry, just send them the check when I could. I think the good Lord was watching out for us.

We struggled on and on, then in 1956, after working eight years at the blouse factory, I gathered up enough courage to ask my boss for a 10 cent an hour raise. His answer was: "Why don't you and Bernie give up that house of yours before you lose it? Bernie is sick most of the time, and the whole burden is on your shoulders." Honest, those were his exact words. I felt he was completely out of line and resented this very much. I decided then and there that I would quit working for him as soon as the lay-off season came early in the summer. You see, the garment business is seasonal, and we could count on at least two lay-offs between seasons, lasting as long as six weeks each. During this summer lay-off, the first two weeks were with pay (or vacation) the rest was just plain lay-off until they started working on the new styles, and call us back.

After making up my mind to quit the blouse factory, I decided I would like to work at Boeing again, and filled out my application there. I made regular visits to the employment office, and each time I was told they could give me office work, but no opening in factory work (which is what I wanted). This went on for about six months, each time the same answer. It was very discouraging, but I wouldn't give up. Then came the summer lay-off, and I was getting desperate. I was still very determined to work for the Boeing Company, and went again to the employment office, only to be told again that there was no factory work to be had. Came home in tears.

Then, suddenly an idea hit me. Why not write a letter to the Boeing Company President himself, telling him that I had worked for Boeing before as a riveter, and how much I enjoyed it there.

So, I sat down and wrote the letter, pouring out my heart and my woes. I repeated the fact that I had worked at Boeing during the war for over three years, and had also maintained a near perfect attendance record. I told him how I had been trying to get a job at Boeing for almost six months, asking for factory or production work. Finally I ended my letter with these words: "A word or a phone call from your office to the Boeing Employment Office is as good as a job for me." Well, just four days after I mailed that letter, I received a phone call from the Boeing Employment Office asking me to come down for a job interview—I rushed down. On the desk in front of the man who interviewed me, was my letter, with a pink "Immediate Attention" attached to it. I was thus duly interviewed, and the very next day started to work at Plant II, in the production line. So, on July 23, 1956, I started my second career at Boeing.

Bernie was feeling pretty good now, and doing more and more work on his own. I was happy with my work at Boeing, and we gradually got back on our feet. We were making regular payments on our home, and even paid off the $600.00 loaned to us by our friends. By 1963 things looked pretty rosy, and we decided to take our first real vacation by going to Hawaii for ten days. How wonderful it all was. It put new life into us. However, we never dreamed at the time of all the heartaches and sickness that was in store for us.

Early in the Spring of 1965 Bernie suffered a slight heart attack and was hospitalized. When he was well enough to come home, I took time off from work to nurse him. It was several months before he could do any kind of work—doctor's orders.

We had about three more years to go before our 15-year mortgage would be paid in full. We were now counting the months when the house would be ours.

Then, one day Bernie had a terrible case of hiccups that wouldn't stop. After two days of this our doctor ordered him to the hospital. None of the known remedies helped, and he lost a lot of weight, and got real weak. After six days of this suffering, the specialists on the case suggested injecting ether under the skin of his right hand, and in five minutes the hiccups stopped. Bernie was very weak from the ordeal, and when he came home, again I took time off from my work to be with him, and to prepare special foods. Boeing was just wonderful about my taking off so much time from work. They let me use my vacation and sick-leave days so that my paychecks could continue coming in.

No sooner was Bernie strong enough to work when he became ill again. Tests showed he had prostate gland problems, and was advised to have surgery. So, back into the hospital for the operation—more time off for me while he recuperated at home. I could see a definite change in Bernie. All of these surgeries were now slowing him down. This only made me love him all the more. I knew all the suffering he had gone through. By now I had given up all hopes of raising a family (I was now in my middle 50's) and devoted my life to caring for Bernie. He needed me, and I loved him so dearly.

In the early Spring of 1968, he became seriously ill again. Not only had he been unable to eat for days, but he was also in severe pain. He woke up in the middle of the night and was practically rolling on the floor with pain. His eyes were sunken into their sockets, and his face was the color of ash. I remember phoning our family doctor at his home at 1:00 o'clock in the morning. The doctor told me to rush him to the Cabrini Hospital to the emergency room, and that he would phone ahead for admittance. After some medications to ease his pain, many tests were done which revealed that he had an adhesion. This is a condition caused when the intestine attaches itself to the thick scar tissue of the stomach lining, causing blockage of the bowels. These scar tissues were caused by the previous surgeries on the stomach and the abdomen that were done in the past. Because this upcoming surgery was of a very serious nature, and because he was so weak going into it, each of us was silently worried, and wondered if he could pull through. Bernie went into the emergency operation at 7:00 o'clock in the evening. I suffered in silence in the waiting room, until the surgeon came up from surgery around midnight to say that Bernie would be okay. He added, however, that he had some very distressing news. During the operation, he had discovered an air bubble in Bernie's aorta, (the main artery) for which there was no cure except surgery. This meant an open-heart surgery—another major operation. Oh Lord, what else, what else? How much suffering can one human being stand? The doctor explained it to me thus: If the bubble is not removed by surgery it will progressively get larger, and will finally break though the lining of the aorta causing severe internal bleeding and instant death. I was warned not to mention this fact to Bernie—he was too weak to stand the news of an open-heart surgery. The doctor said he would break the news himself, when Bernie got a little stronger. I kept this secret locked in my heart for six long months, and it was sheer torture.

Bernie took a long time recovering. Again, I took time off from work. I will never forget just how wonderful Boeing was about it. Even my general supervisor told me not to worry about losing my job, and to take off as many days as was necessary, but to be sure to phone in every morning.

In July, 1968, the doctor told Bernie about the air bubble and the necessity of its removal. Poor Bernie was shocked. He agreed to go to the hospital in September. You see, in August our 15-year mortgage would finally be paid off, and we had planned a little party. This house was paid for with blood, sweat, and tears. Although we liked our house very much, it seemed as though it had brought us a lot of sickness and hardship.

About the middle of August we had our little "Mortgage Burning Party" on our patio and the large back yard. It was a beautiful Sunday, with about 40 guests—friends, neighbors, and about a dozen boys and girls from Boeing. Bernie had a huge sign made which read: "The Cohen Hilton—It's All Ours." He had it draped across our grape arbor, visible for blocks. There was a spread of a buffet lunch and beverages. Cameras were snapping all over the place. There was laughter on everyone's lips. What a happy day that was!

Toward the end of September, 1968, Bernie entered the Cabrini Hospital for his open-heart surgery, which was considered a serious major operation. The damaged part of the aorta with the air-bubble was to be cut out, and the section replaced by a piece of Teflon tubing, to allow the blood to continue to flow.

At 7:00 a.m., as they were wheeling Bernie down the corridor to surgery, he held my hand, and with tears in his eyes said, "Mama, I love you." I think this was the first time in all our married years that I ever saw him cry. Needless to say there were tears in my eyes too. I think we both were worried about this operation. I waited in his room for what seemed an eternity, praying all the time for his successful surgery. They finally brought Bernie up around noon. I sat there holding his hand and praying all day. He opened his eyes towards evening and seeing me there, groggily said, "Mama, I love you." I cannot begin to tell you the countless hours and days I spent at his bedside through all his illnesses and operations over the years. Like a magnet, I was drawn closer and closer to him, and I just couldn't do enough for him. I loved him so dearly. God gave us both the courage and strength to withstand each ordeal.

At this time, our Silver Wedding Anniversary was only three and a half months away and, as an incentive, I promised to take him to Acapulco, Mexico in January, if he was well and strong enough to travel by then. The doctor was very pleased with Bernie's progress, and approved of our trip. On January 16th, 1969, we flew down to Acapulco for six days.

I can't help feeling that the last two serious operations Bernie had really stripped him of all his strength. He tired easily, and was talking about retiring. Of course, I encouraged him on this, and in June, 1970, at the age of 62, he went into total retirement, and applied for his Social Security.

Meanwhile, I continued with my job at Boeing. I was transferred to the Electronic Manufacturing Facilities Building and was working with electronic parts. I was still in the Minute-Man Space Program, but the work was entirely different than anything I had done before. I felt lost and confused. Lady Luck was with me. My lead-girl took great pains to teach me the work. Yes, good old Mary (Templeton)! She was a hard working girl with many duties of her own. But, busy as she was, she would never hesitate to stop what she was doing and help me with my problems, or explain something I didn't understand. She truly had the patience of a Saint.

Eventually I got into the swing of things, and put my whole heart into my work, giving it my very best.

At this point, it had now been fourteen years since I was re-hired by Boeing in 1956. My husband had already taken an early retirement because of his health, and was now at home all alone (for a year now). I was inwardly considering taking an early retirement myself so I could be with him, and take care of him. I worried about Bernie constantly. I decided to work two more years, then retire at the age of 62 and collect 80 percent of my Social Security. I concentrated on my job and worked hard. The days and months flew by. In the Fall of 1972, I completed the last few details of my Social Security set-up, and was told that I would receive my first check in February, 1973.

Early in December, 1972, I gave notice of my intention to terminate in January, 1973 and go into retirement. My Supervisor, Patrick Flaherty, wasn't too happy about it, and tried to persuade me to stay on another year or two. Poor Pat. How he tried. But, how could I? I was now 62 years old, had already set up my Social Security and, above all, had promised my Bernie I would retire and take care of him. I wouldn't disappoint him now for anything in the world. True, we would suffer financially, as I was earning good wages at Boeing for which I was so grateful. Only a person who had worked in a sweat shop for as many years as I have, can really appreciate working in a place like Boeing. There were so many factors to consider. I had been working since I was 14 years old, doing house work while putting myself through school, then working in a sweat shop—mostly on piece work—struggling for a mere existence, living from hand to mouth, as the saying goes. My only decent wage was earned while working at Boeing, even though I was in a low wage category. Now, at 62 years old, I had put behind me 48 years of hard work.

I set Friday, January 26, 1973, as my final day at Boeing. That week the ball started to roll, and various paper works were filled out and signed. Even now, Pat, my Supervisor, was trying to persuade me to re-consider, telling me the job was mine for as long as I wanted it. But ———

The final day arrived, and with it an empty and sad feeling in my heart. I looked all around me, and realized that this day I would leave them all—all my friends. Pat said I wasn't to work at all that day, but to take it easy, for this was my day. What a jewel he was. And my lead girl Mary—who but Mary would think of presenting me with a beautiful pink and white carnation corsage done up in pink and silver ribbons? She was another jewel.

Then came the lunch period—an occasion to be remembered the rest of my life. A long table was laden with brightly wrapped gifts, and a large cake beautifully decorated with the words "Happy Retirement Naomi." There was a large urn filled with coffee, and stacks of paper napkins and plates to be served with the cake to everyone. Speeches were made, and pictures taken. The one gift that will always be cherished, and will always hang in the place of honor in our living room, is a huge framed picture signed by over a hundred persons—all people I worked with. This picture is far from ordinary. In the center were two pictures in a circle, one showing Bernie and me at our wedding some thirty years ago, and the other as we were now. These two pictures were surrounded by pictures of seven different models of airplanes and a missile (that Boeing had built, and I had worked on parts on all of them). The whole project was my Supervisor Pat's idea. I'm sure he must have gone through a lot of planning and time to have it done, signed and framed. Of course, Bernie was there too, with his wonderful sense of humor. He had brought a huge purple velvet heart, which he pinned on me, saying I deserved a purple heart for putting up with him through all these years. Everyone laughed and applauded. It all soon came to an end. Lunch was over, and everyone returned to work. Bernie and I lingered on for a while saying good-bye. Finally we gathered up all the gifts, put them in our car and left. There was a twinge of pain in my heart about leaving the place. It was as though I was leaving a part of my heart behind. I promised then and there that I would come back periodically—with Bernie— to visit my friends.

At home now, it was nearing dinner time. Bernie suggested that we eat out since this was my retirement day. I agreed. He said he was going to take me to a real nice restaurant, and away we drove down the Pacific Highway South. When we finally arrived, the biggest surprise of my life was waiting for me. Bernie was in on this surprise. There were banquet tables set up, and so many of my friends and coworkers were there, milling around, waiting for us. There were even a few boys I knew who were working in other plants, and whom I hadn't seen for several years. Somehow, they got there for the banquet (I guess the whole affair was arranged by Pat). Even my General Supervisor and his wife were there. It was hard to believe that all of these people were there to honor me with a banquet. Bernie was in his glory when Pat asked him to be the Master of Ceremonies and to tell a few of his jokes. (I was fighting back tears of joy.) Then, to top it all, I was presented with my 20 Year service pin with tiny diamonds on it—even though I was short about four months of 20 years. Again, as if all this wasn't enough, a week later Boeing News came out with a wonderful story on me, complete with my picture, and a review of my almost 20 years of service at Boeing. Yes, it was a wonderful day to remember all of my life. We came home about 9:00 p.m., and there was yet more surprises waiting for me. A huge, gorgeous, fresh flower arrangement sent by wire from our dear friends in Hope, Idaho. The following day, two more beautiful potted flowers arrived with cards from our dear friends in Edmonds, Washington, and from our God-daughter and her husband in Everett, Washington. As Bernie and I sat around talking about the last two days events, he put his arms around me and said, "Gee, Mama, I never realized how much those people at Boeing loved you."

Having retired, now I had to adjust myself to a new way of living. For the first time in 48 years I didn't have to set the alarm clock to wake me up at 5:00 am. How wonderful it was going to be to sleep in as late as I wanted for the rest of my life. Gradually I got accustomed to this easy way of living. I kept busy with yard and house work. Evenings Bernie and I watched television or played cards.

I must not forget to mention, that for quite some time now, Bernie had been prodding me into learning to drive a car. I wasn't interested in the idea much because I was so deathly afraid of traffic. Bernie kept on and on, and finally I thought why not give it a try. I took it as a big challenge, and contacted a driving school. After eight lessons I took the test and failed. In fact, I failed several times, but wouldn't give up, having come this far. Finally I received my driver's license of which I was very proud. Now, to the average person learning to drive is no big deal—even teenagers drive. But to me it was a very big deal, considering the fact that I was 62 years old and that I was only 4'10" tall. Believe me, it took a lot of nerve on my part to take up this challenge, but I was glad now that I did. Needless to say, I surprised a lot of my friends.

In May, 1973, soon after I retired, Bernie had a yearning to go to Hawaii again—this time to go up the river Kauai on the Island of Kauai, to the beautiful Fern Grotto, and repeat our wedding vows in celebration of our forthcoming 30th Anniversary, which was in January.

On May 16, 1973, we got on board the wonderful, giant, super-jet Boeing 747, and started the flight over the Pacific Ocean to Hawaii. Oh what a beautiful, awesome, huge plane, holding a maximum capacity of 360 passengers. Superb meals were served the passengers, to say nothing of the between meal snacks, and movies for entertainment. I couldn't believe all this was happening to me.

We arrived in Honolulu. Four days later we flew to the Island of Maui, to visit a Seattle friend who had made her permanent home there. From Maui we flew to the Island of Kauai and finally by boat to the beautiful Fern Grotto, to repeat our wedding vows. It was a real Hawaiian wedding, complete with a Hawaiian minister, witnesses, a marriage certificate, dancers, etc. There were several natives playing their guitars and singing the beautiful Hawaiian Wedding Song. We would remember this event as one of the highlights of our life.

Two years have already flown by since my retirement. Bernie and I live peacefully in our modest, little one-bedroom home. We are both in our 60's. The almost half-century of hard work and struggle have left their permanent marks on me. My hair has turned practically all gray, I am round shouldered, and my face is sprinkled with tell-tale wrinkles. Yes, it has been a hard life, but I thank God that my struggles were in a blessed country like AMERICA, where anyone who wants to work for a living has a chance (unlike the barbaric and ravaged Turkey where I was born). YES INDEED. I also thank God for blessing me with such excellent health. Thus, I look around me, flanked by my two pet cats, the color T.V., the comfortable furniture, and above all, my wonderful husband, and

Naomi's Story

again, I count my blessings. I ask myself "why, why, did God choose to save ME from among my family of eight, and bring me to this wonderful country, and give me all this? I was no better than the rest of them." Then once more, my thoughts and memories race back some 58 torturous years to Marash, Turkey, to the terrible year of 1917, as they had every single day of my life since, when on that fateful Saturday in June, my entire family was driven into exile by the Turks, along with hundreds of other Armenian families. That Saturday had become a total obsession with me—how I was snatched away from my family just before their departure—never even said good-bye—and, then later to the orphanage, pushed in through the door—with no words spoken—and, where I remained for almost five years. My eyes would slowly fill with hot tears, and run down my cheeks. Sensing what was going through my mind, my wonderful husband Bernie, being the kind person that he was, understands and softly slips an arm around my shoulders, and without a word, lets me cry it out. I guess the terribly lonely, empty and aching feeling in my heart will always be with me, forever tormenting me. Until I die, I will always wonder what happened to my family, how they died (if indeed they all died) and in what part of the world. I am sure that without Bernie, my life would have been utterly unbearable. He brought sunshine and happiness to my life, with his happy-go-lucky personality and priceless sense of humor, not to mention a heart as big as the world itself. Yes, Bernie was good for me. He taught me how to smile again. He truly dried my tears to a great extent.

The eight major operations, and a heart attack during the last 15 some years had gradually drained all of Bernie's strength. He now spends his days laying on the davenport all day, watching television or napping—going out only occasionally. I keep busy with my house and yard work, shopping, cooking, etc. and looking after his needs. Our doors are always open to welcome our friends.

It is now the year 1976. We have been married for over 32 years, and deeply in love. Thus we spend our twilight years, living each day quietly in our modest little "love nest", trusting in God, with peace and contentment. We are truly grateful for the many wonderful friends we have. We count our blessings each day..

Epilogue

As I have mentioned in the foregoing of my autobiography, I consider myself very fortunate and lucky to be living in blessed America. In fact, on occasion, I have felt an uncontrollable urge to get down on my knees and kiss the ground—I am that grateful to be in this country. And yet, even though the memory of the horrible events I witnessed, and even went through in Marash, Turkey, are forever locked in my heart, so are locked in my heart some of the pleasant things I still remember and cherish.

I would be untrue to myself, and a liar, if I didn't say that part of my heart is still there, and always will be. I cannot escape this. There are times when I long to be back there, but this feeling comes over me only when I remember the happy and pleasant things. Though the city of Marash, Turkey, where I was born, was a beautiful city, the Turks had made it a hell on earth for us Armenian Christians. I have no desire whatsoever to go back there—even for a visit. I shall endeavor to forget the horrible events, if possible, and remember only the few pleasant things so dear to my heart.

And so, for this reason, I have tried to duplicate a few of these happy memories here in our home, in America.

First, there in our beautiful back yard is a gorgeous fig tree, with its large, green shiny leaves, giving us an abundance of luscious, sweet figs each year. It is a sheer joy to me.

Next is our beautiful grape arbor that my wonderful husband built for me, because I once mentioned to him how I longed for a grape arbor like the ones we had in the old country. This arbor serves tri-fold—it gives us sweet red grapes, provides us with delightful shade to sit in during the hot summer afternoons, and lastly, I use its leaves to stuff with rice, tomatoes, meat and lemon juice, for a delicious meal. We call it Sarma. I remember my mother making this for us all through the summer months, because we all loved it so. It is one of the most popular foods in our part of the country.

How can I overlook mentioning my wonderful climbing Honeysuckle vine, so full of yellow and cream-colored flowers, sending forth such delicate fragrance filling the gentle, cool evening breeze. It is a sheer delight to behold this amazing climber, where the humming birds build their nest.

It would be a sin not to include one of my most treasured climbers in our beautiful back yard, namely the Night Blooming Jasmine. One has but to see this wonderful plant to appreciate and to love it, with its tiny, white clusters of flowers, lacy leaves, sending forth such intoxicating fragrance, filling the cool night air. My one great regret is that I could not get a Mulberry tree too.

Last, but not the least by any means, comes my real pride and joy, my wonderful, wonderful sleeping balcony. One day as I was sitting under the grape arbor, looking through green leaves to the blue skies above, I casually mentioned to my husband that I wished we had a sleeping balcony built right off the ground where I could sleep under the open skies during the warm summer nights. Being the wonderful man that he was, he agreed, and left the whole project up to me, saying go ahead and pick a spot, plan how it was to be built, right off one of our bedroom windows, and facing our lovely back yard. I planned to have this balcony built so that my Night Blooming Jasmine was on one end and my tall, majestic and graceful Weeping Willow tree on the other. Thus, as I lie in bed on my balcony, looking up at the twinkling stars above, and breathing in the intoxicating fragrance of the Jasmine, and the night air gently stirring in the breeze by the nearby swaying Weeping Willow branches, I could imagine myself once more back in Marash, Turkey, laying on our veranda, under the huge Mulberry tree, surrounded by my family. Then my life in Turkey goes through my mind once more, and the tears start again, wondering what became of them.

Regardless of the tears, I hope that the few pleasant things I remember, and have duplicated in my home, will help me to forget the many sad, unpleasant and terrible things that I still remember so well.

* * *

It is now early in the year 1977, which was to be the blackest year of my life. Even though Bernie had been sick during most of our married life, and had survived eight operations, early in March, 1977, he was struck down with infection of the gall bladder, and had to go back to Cabrini Hospital. At this time he weighed only 109 pounds and was too weak to have the gall bladder removed by surgery. He did not respond to medical treatment, and on March 3, 1977, on Thursday morning at 3:10 a.m., Bernie passed on to a better world at the age of 68. At last he was at eternal peace, where there is no pain, no agony, no surgeries.

In Bernie's Will, he had requested that the song "I'll Be Loving You Always" be sung at his funeral. As my beloved Bernie lay so peacefully in the casket, our song was being sung, accompanied on the organ ever so softly. The funeral hall was filled to its capacity with his friends who loved and adored him. There wasn't a dry eye in the place. This song had been our theme song during our entire married life and had been played at our wedding 33 years ago. I think this was Bernie's way of saying good-bye to me. I was in the mourners' room crying uncontrollably, while my aching heart was slowly dying inches inside of me. This was the blackest hour of my entire life. Oh, the tears I shed following his death during all the nights, days, weeks and months that followed. He was the one ray of sunshine in my life. He had taught me how to smile again, and had truly dried my tears—tears that I had shed before he came into my life. When he died, he took that one ray of sunshine with him, leaving me in darkness again. With his passing on, leaving me behind, my world crumpled all around me and stopped turning.

Feelings from my Heart

So our happy married life together for 33 years and 45 days came to an end. I am now 66 years old, and once again completely alone except, of course, for my many wonderful friends—in particular, the wonderful McGill family.

I go to visit my husband's grave with fresh flowers as often as I can, say a silent prayer, and shed a few tears. Then I come home to an empty house, empty, but filled with ever so many fond memories, memories that are forever locked in my heart, and cry some more. Life without him is very lonely—so terribly lonely that at times it is almost beyond endurance. My heart is filled with sorrow and pain, and part of that heart is in the grave with him. I will grieve for him till the day I die.

My eternal resting place is next to his grave, with one long marker over both graves, when the divine Lord above is ready to beckon me to join my beloved husband. Only then will my lonely and aching heart find peace.

My Prayer

God grant me the serenity to accept the things I cannot change, the courage to change the things I can, and the wisdom to know the difference. God's will be done. Amen.

—This is the very true story of my life. Everything I have seen and gone through is true, and will live in my memory until I die. So ends my story as of March, 1977.

Naomi Nuritza Kalemjian Cohen (Mrs. Bernie Cohen)

Naomi's Album

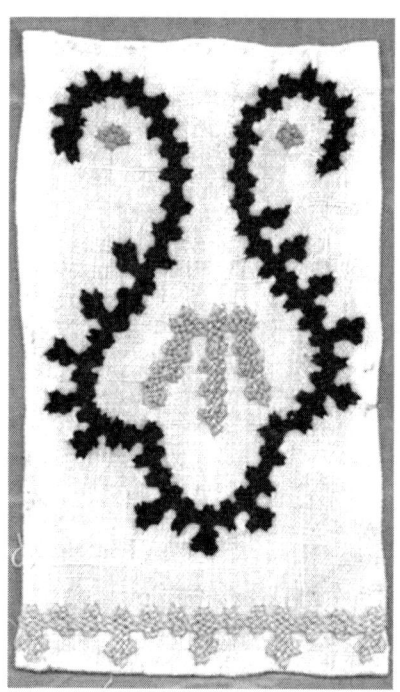

Samples of Armenian Lace and Weaving as done by the orphans.

74   Naomi's Story

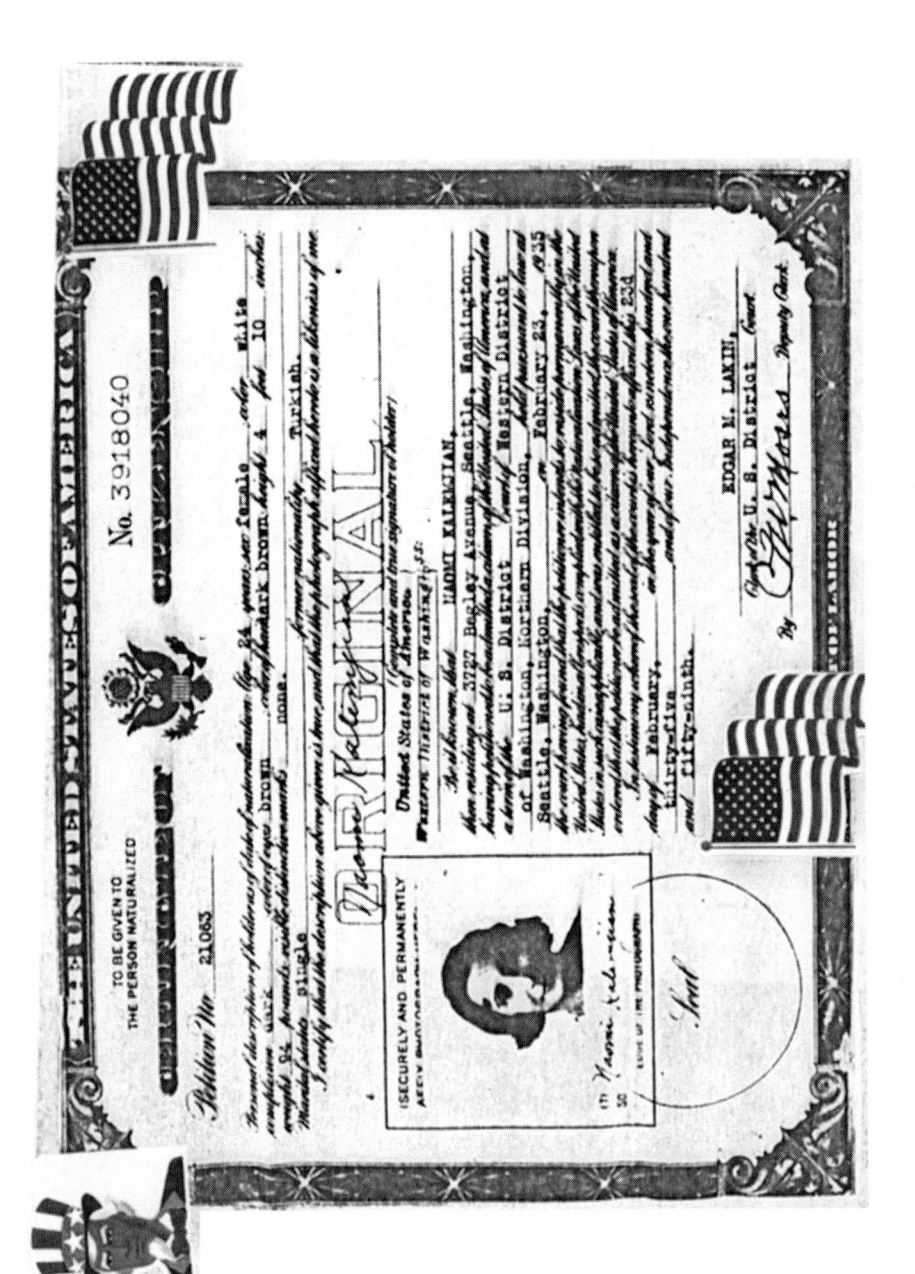

Naomi's dearest possession was her citizenship paper.

Naomi's Story 75

below: Mrs. M. Krikoriam, Naomi's aunt who paid her way to Seattle and J.E. Mather who helped her escape from Turkey.

Naomi with her two little cousins in Beirut before she sailed for the United States. All were orphans.

Girl Travels 10,000 Seattle

Partial reprint from Seattle P.I. Newspaper, Nov. 26, 1922.

Naomi at her Aunt's home shortly after her arrival. Seattle PI photo

Naomi's Story 77

Naomi Kalemjian, July, 1936, while visiting some friends at their home.

Naomi N. Kalemjian

Mr. and Mrs. D. Korkegian
request the honor of your presence
at the marriage of their niece
Naomi N. Kalemjian
to
Mr. Bernard S. Cohen
on Sunday, the sixteenth of January
Nineteen hundred and forty-four
eight o'clock in the evening
at the Temple De Hirsch
Fifteenth and East Union
Seattle, Washington

Reception to follow
in the Church Hall

Presenting
Mr. and Mrs. Bernard S. Cohen

The bride and groom, Bernie and Naomi N. Cohen, on their wedding day.
January 16, 1944.
"We continued holding hands until he died."

Naomi's Story

My Secret Love

To My Darling Wife!

I have a secret to tell you
A secret I know that's true:
That you're like a rose in the garden,
With its fragrance as lovely as you.

A lifetime is loaded with secrets.
Many have never been told,
But the one that I'm telling you, darling,
Is worth more than a mountain of gold.

The raindrops fall from the heavens
To water the flowers below.
And our love is sprinkled with blessings
Like a rose in the garden that grows.

My dear, you're worth more than a million.
In my heart you have played the star part.
I will always call you, "My darling!"
For you are the queen of my heart.

Composed by Henry Vanney

With all my Love Bernie!!
Sept 6, 1970

Naomi's wedding party was arranged by Bernie who loved her so much and courted her extravagantly for those lean war-time years. Years later he wrote her the poem, "My Secret Love."

Photos from Naomi's album

Our little "Love Nest", Aug. 13, 1953

At last—there goes the old mortgage on the house—August 1968

Naomi's Story

Their Appetites will Make the Axis Burp

Bernie Cohen in center of photo serving "Axis" salad to Boeing employees to promote sales of War Bonds and stamps. (Boeing News Weekly 12/3/43)

The airplane that made Boeing and won the war. the first B-17

BOEING GOES TO WAR

Naomi's Retirement Party
February 22, 1973

Our Rosie the Riveter Retires

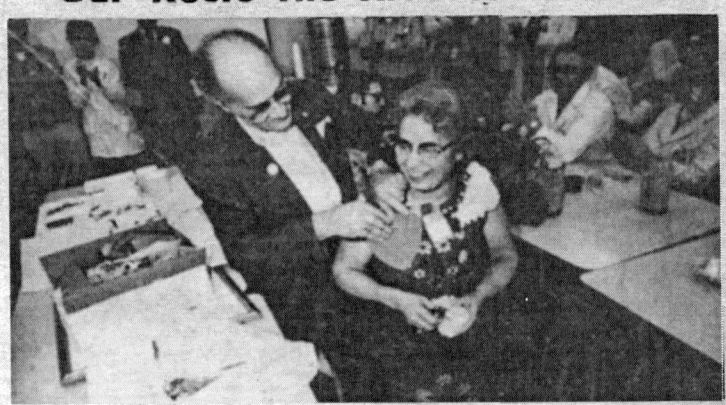

Naomi Cohen, the World War 2 riveter who once wrote a letter to William M. Allen for help in returning to Boeing, has retired. Naomi, a dispatcher in electronics, is shown above as fellow employees feted her at a going-away party.

Another Link With War Is Gone; Naomi Now Can Sleep Past Dawn

A tiny woman with a lot of spirit has retired from Boeing.

She is Naomi Cohen, Boeing Electronics factory dispatcher, who was a riveter during World War 2. The last B-17 to leave Seattle had the skin of its nose section completely riveted, compliments of Naomi.

The Boeing News during World War 2 turned society paper to cover the wedding of Naomi and Bernie Cohen, Boeing electrician. The reception for hundreds of Boeing employees was held in the Plant 2 cafeteria. The wedding gift from the BOEING NEWS staff to the bride and bridegroom was a scrapbook of the wedding complete with a hand-drawn cover showing two entwined hearts.

Naomi also had a part in Bernie's schemes to pep up sales of war savings stamps in the Boeing factory. These well-publicized stunts of World War 2 involved burning the stamps, plastering them over a life-size figure of Herman Goering and mixing them into a "give the Axis indigestion" salad.

Naomi also wrote a long letter to William M. Allen when he was president of the company. When World War 2 came to its abrupt end, Naomi's riveting job disappeared. Ten years later she decided she wanted to become a Boeing employee again.

After six months of visits to the Boeing employment office with no action, she says, "I got tired. So I sat down and wrote a letter to Mr. Allen telling him that I wanted to come back, that Boeing was a pretty good place to work and that I had a perfect attendance record. I remember writing Mr. Allen that a telephone call from his office to the employment office was as good as a job. Four days later the employment office called and here I am now retiring."

For most of the past 16 years in her second career with Boeing, Naomi has been a shop clerk in Minuteman production.

"In a way I regret retiring," Naomi said, "but my husband Bernie is ill and I should be at home."

What is she going to do in retirement? "I'm very happy. I've got my husband and my home and I'm going to stay home. I'm going to work on my autobiography and finish the last half of it."

Naomi, an Armenian born in Turkey, lost her family during World War 1. An aunt living in the U.S. found her through the Red Cross as a 12-year-old girl living in a Turkish orphanage and brought her to this country.

"I've been working for 48 years," she said, "ever since I was 14, and the best years have been the years I've worked at Boeing."

Naomi's Story

Naomi's Retirement Party
January 26, 1973

Naomi's Supervisor hands her a picture-plaque with hundreds of her fellow workers' signatures and well-wishes as Bernie looks on.

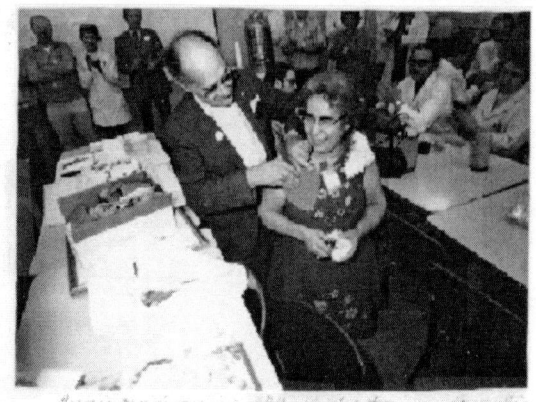

Bernie pins his "Purple Heart" on Naomi for "putting up with him so long."

Naomi mourns Bernie